658.8   Foster, Dennis L.
FC

   The complete
   franchise book

$17.95

© THE BAKER & TAYLOR CO.

The Complete
Franchise Book

How to Order:

Quantity discounts are available from Prima Publishing & Communications, Post Office Box 1260DF, Rocklin, CA 95677; Telephone: (916) 624-5718. On your letterhead, include information concerning the intended use of the books and the number of books you wish to purchase.

THE COMPLETE FRANCHISE BOOK

**What You Must Know
(And Are Rarely Told)
About Buying or Starting
Your Own Franchise**

Dennis L. Foster

Prima Publishing and Communications
Post Office Box 1260DF
Rocklin, California 95677
Telephone: (916) 624-5718

Editors: Suzanne Mikesell and Brian Wilson
Cover Design: Dunlavey Studios

Prima Publishing & Communications
P.O. Box 1260DF
Rocklin, CA 95677
(916) 624-5718

Library of Congress Cataloging-in-Publication Data

Foster, Dennis L.

The complete franchise book.

Bibliography: p.

Includes index.

1. Franchises (Retail trade) I. Title.

HF5429.23.F67 1987   658.8'708   87-2471

ISBN 0-914629-24-7

88 89 90 91   10 9 8 7 6 5 4 3 2 1

Printed in the United States of America by:
R.R. Donnelley & Sons Company

Contents

Section III: FRANCHISING IN ACTION

APPENDICES

Why You Need to Read This Book

The word "franchise" has come to mean many things. Mention the term to a pro football scout and he'll think you mean a "franchise" player who can take a team from the cellar to the Super Bowl simply by signing. Mention franchising to an attorney and immediately he thinks in terms of caveats and covenants. A politician might think you're referring to the right to vote in a public election. Most of us, though, imagine double-decker burgers on sesame-seed buns, crispy fried drumsticks, and steamy pizzas. Fast food is easily the most visible manifestation of franchising in American life.

But how many Americans, I wonder, know that Coca-Cola is a franchised product, as are Ford, Hertz, and the New York Yankees? We encounter the face of franchising every time we open a refrigerator door, or drive down a city street. Everywhere — on signs, on stores, on billboards and truck panels — franchise names permeate daily life.

But mention franchising to me and most likely I *won't* think of a Heisman-winning quarterback, an instant hot lunch, or even a complicated business contract. The first thing I'll probably visualize is Tom Sawyer offering Huck Finn a franchise to whitewash his aunt's fence.

When Tom convinced Huck to fork over money and valuables for the "privilege" of taking up Tom's labor, he was indeed selling a small business franchise. Tom used a now-famous marketing technique called "reverse selling," in which the customer and salesman exchange roles. To get Huck to assume the nasty whitewashing job, Tom had to make

1

his friend *want* the job, by cultivating an irresistible motivation to obtain the "privilege." Yet, when he finally convinced Tom to sell him the franchise, far from begrudging Tom for playing such a trick, Huck derived real gratification from the job. His pleasure was based on the fact that he had *paid* for the franchise and, in effect, "owned" the whitewashing privilege.

This famous incident has a great deal to do with modern franchising. Like Tom Sawyer, a franchisor attracts and motivates franchisees by dangling "karats" — catering to basic human desires for financial independence and personal achievement. But if as cash-paying franchisees we did not derive satisfaction — not to mention profits — from our franchises, the whole idea would vanish from the scene as fast as a "franchise" quarterback with bad knees.

The issue of the psychological bonds between franchisor and franchisee is ignored in most other books and magazines about franchising. Yet these bonds constitute the heart and soul of franchising. Besides attention to the obvious financial and legal aspects of a franchise, success demands a delicate balance among the psychological, sociological, and emotional ingredients.

This book was written, in part, to fill that gap by exploring the myriad subtle relationships that underlie a successful association between a franchisor and a franchisee. Many of these relationships come into play long before an agreement is struck and the franchise is sold. Understanding these subtle relationships is paramount to researching, evaluating, and negotiating a franchise purchase; more importantly, it's essential to succeeding in the business.

If you have ever seen another book or magazine article about franchising, you know there are other sources that can tell you where to find franchise opportunities and what questions to ask a franchisor. In fact, because this book is titled *The Complete Franchise Book*, that kind of information is also covered here. But this book really begins where those others leave off: with the premise of *being successful in a franchise business*. It's not enough simply to know where franchisors are listed, or how to evaluate a franchisor's credentials. You need to know the factors and forces that will influence your success as a franchise owner — beginning with the moment you first decide to look into it.

As a consultant in franchising, I'm approached for assistance by both franchisors and would-be franchisees. In these pages, I answer the questions most often raised by those contemplating a franchise investment. One of the most interesting things about consulting is the rich exchange of information that occurs. One cannot help learning something valuable from every teaching experience, particularly when one's students are successful entrepreneurs and industrialists. Sharing some of the insights gained from those exchanges is another reason for this book.

I would like to take this opportunity to acknowledge and thank Jim Ullman, franchise attorney *extraordinaire*, for being kind enough to review the sections dealing with legal and regulatory issues. Jim possesses a broad range of legal experiences in franchising, both domestic and international.

To place franchising in a practical light, this book is heavily sprinkled with case histories, anecdotes, and examples. In a few the real name(s) of the people and companies involved are used. In most cases, the names have been changed to protect the author and publisher against the vehement outcries — or worse — of the guilty. In some examples, even the industry has been changed to further disguise the identities of the parties. If, by coincidence, you run across a person or company with the same or a similar name as one of the fictitious names in this book — e.g., SuperFat Franchise Corporation or Rosy Futures, Inc. — please be assured there is no connection whatsoever.

When I refer to franchisors and franchisees in this book, I use the masculine pronoun merely for convenience; all the principles and statements apply to females as well as males.

Smoothing the Road to Business Success

One crisp morning in spring, an entrepreneur, whom we'll call Andrew, opened a modest, forty-room motor inn right off Route 66, just outside Flagstaff, Arizona. He picked the location himself, hoping to attract vacationing families and traveling salesmen. By the time he finished building and furnishing the motel, he had little money left for advertising and public relations. Andrew's intention was to let his big, bright electric sign do all the advertising, blinking its neon message to passing motorists twenty-four hours a day.

But as the months passed, Andrew had a tough time filling his forty rooms. The motel seemed to have all the right things going for it: it was brand new, the location was terrific, and it had the biggest illuminated sign on the block. Yet, time after time, motorists would drive right by Andrew's place only to turn into an older, less visible motor inn down the street.

Today, only ten months after opening his door for business, Andrew's motel is up for sale.

The motel down the block was owned by a businesswoman whom we'll call Andrea. Like Andrew, Andrea was a small-time independent — but unlike him, she was not *totally* independent. She started her motel by purchasing a franchise from a well-known lodging organization.

Andrea's franchisor helped her select a site for the motor inn based on the company's prior experience in the lodging business. They knew things about attracting customers it would take Andrew years to learn on his own. After three weeks of intensive training at franchise headquarters, Andrea shared much of that know-how.

Andrea's motel had fifty-five rooms, compared to Andrew's forty. Yet she constructed and attractively furnished it for about a third less than what it cost Andrew to build his. How? Andrea's franchisor had already negotiated low prices from suppliers based on projected orders from a large number of franchisees. As a result, Andrea paid wholesale prices for the same items that Andrew had to buy at retail.

The franchise agreement called for Andrea to pay a small percentage of her monthly income into a co-operative advertising fund. By itself, this meager contribution was of little value in promoting her motel. But, combined with similar contributions from the other two hundred or so franchises in the organization, Andrea's payment helped finance a national television campaign, full-page advertisements in major business and travel magazines, and prominent listings in every major hotel guide. Andrew couldn't afford even a small ad in one of these magazines and had to content himself with free listings in a few travel pamphlets.

In spite of their physical similarities, Andrew's motel went under in less than a year while Andrea's continues to thrive to this day. She's even thinking about opening a second franchise in Bakersfield, California.

Andrea's example points out some of the advantages you might enjoy as the owner of a franchise business. The example of Andrew, her unsuccessful competitor, illustrates some of the risks you would encounter by going it on your own.

The Department of Commerce reports that fewer than three percent of the nation's franchises fail each year. Compare that to the Small Business Administration statistic that eighty percent of all private enterprises eventually fail, most of them in the first year. Is it any wonder that interest in franchising is at an all-time high?

Still, in all the excitement and enthusiasm, it's easy to overlook some of the potential perils of the franchise trade. Here's another case history, with a similar beginning but a very different outcome.

On a sultry August day in Florida a cafeteria worker, whom we'll call Jerry, decided to quit his job of seven years and buy a franchise to open a family-style steak house. To swing the deal, he withdrew his life savings, borrowed from a well-to-do aunt, and mortgaged his modest house in the suburbs of Coral Gables.

He knew food service, but nothing about running a business. A month at franchise training school taught him more about running a steak house than he had ever suspected there was to know.

Thanks to heavy promotion on local TV and radio, Jerry's restaurant opened to a rush of business from local residents, as well as tourists.

One day a few months later, the franchise company's field auditor paid Jerry's steak house a visit. After a day-long inspection, the auditor found an unsightly smudge on a mirror in the men's room. Jerry received a written citation notifying him of a default under his franchise agreement. The industrious franchisee hastily washed and polished the mirror himself. Exactly a month later, the field auditor returned for a surprise inspection. To Jerry's horror, the auditor found another smudge, this time on the mirror in the women's room.

The following morning, the franchise company moved to terminate the franchise and seize the restaurant.

Today, the franchisor in Jerry's case might have a difficult time terminating his franchise simply for two smudges on bathroom mirrors. Yet every year some franchisors use excuses every bit as trivial in an attempt to intimidate, harass, or even expel franchisees. By exercising overbearing authority, some merely want to keep their franchisees in line. But undoubtedly a few are interested in taking over the outlets, built from the ground up on franchisees' time, money, and hard work.

Franchising is a dual-edged sword. At its best, it is the entrepreneur's finest hour, a time for transforming simple ideas and bold ambitions into fulfilled dreams of personal enrichment and financial independence. At its worst, it is "vulture capitalism" run amok, in which every conceivable type of quick-buck scam and pyramid sales scheme is foisted on an unsuspecting public. The difference is often less visible than the writing on an oral contract.

This book will help you sort out the facts about franchising and distinguish the signposts of success from the danger signals of failure or fraud. It begins with a broad self-evaluation of your mental, physical, and financial preparedness for franchising and concludes with a systematic procedure for evaluating a franchise opportunity.

Each chapter includes a set of self-tests, checklists, or work sheets to help you organize your search for the perfect franchisor and the ideal franchise opportunity.

We'll examine just what franchisors can — and can't — do to influence you to sign an agreement. We'll also take an in-depth look at the processes of researching the field, applying for a franchise, and preparing for the tough negotiations ahead. You'll learn about the psychological strategies franchisors use to sell their franchises, then find out how to turn the tables to your own advantage.

We'll explore the mysterious regions of the Uniform Franchise Offering Circular (UFOC), translating its terminology into plain English, then dissect a franchise agreement to see how it affects your rights as a business owner. Finally, we'll examine the critical factors that will guide your search, influence your decision, and determine your success.

Along the way, this book will help you answer the following questions:

- Is franchising right for me?
- How can I find the right franchisor for my own personality, objectives, and skills?
- How can I avoid franchise come-ons and rip-offs?
- How can I negotiate the most favorable franchise agreement?
- What should I look for in the franchisor's background?
- What kind of earnings can I realistically expect?
- What are my rights as a franchisee?
- What are my obligations?
- How can I raise the money to build and develop the business?
- What steps can I take to optimize my chances for success?

Use this book to guide you on an even path to the franchise dream of self-management, financial independence, and personal fulfillment.

Section One

Anatomy of a Franchise

"We shall begin in a small way and go on to a large. In any case, it will get us our living and we shall get back our capital."

Fyodor Dostoevsky
Crime and Punishment

Chapter One

What the Red Queen Told Alice

A Strategy for Growth

In *Through the Looking Glass*, the Red Queen tells Alice:

> Here, it takes all the running you can do just to remain
> in the same place. If you want to get someplace else,
> you must run at least twice as fast as that!

Maybe you feel like that sometimes, running as fast as you can just to stay in the same place. When you work for someone else, that's usually about all you can expect. Have you ever wished you were your own boss? Have you thought about owning a profitable small business? Maybe you already own a business but, like the Red Queen and Alice, it's all you can do just to keep the doors open. Have you ever wondered how your business could compete successfully against industry giants? If you can answer "yes" to any of these questions, you're a prime candidate to buy or start your own franchise.

Franchising is a method of owning a business in cooperation with others. It is also a major contributor to the U.S. economy. More importantly, franchising is a strategy for personal and financial growth.

The word "franchise" is almost synonymous with dramatic growth. Today's franchises account for more than a third of the total U.S. retail economy, nearly $700 billion each year. In its publication *Franchising in the Economy*, the Industry and Trade Administration of the U.S. Department of Commerce calls franchising a "phenomenal" influence.

The Franchise Formula

The franchise is America's unique economic relationship. It weds a successful big business to a small-time independent, creating a dynamic relationship between established know-how and the entrepreneurial spirit.

In this respect, a franchise is a mutual success formula, an interdependency in which each party's success rides on the other's. The "franchise" is a right or privilege to conduct a particular business using a specified trade name. Trade secrets and a packaged business format are usually part of the deal. The "franchisor" is the person or company who offers the franchise to others. The person who buys a franchise from a franchisor is the "franchisee." On one hand, the packaged formula equips a franchisor to enter new geographical markets quickly. On the other hand, the relationship offers a small-time operator independence, a ready-made format for a business, and a strong likelihood of survival.

For the benefits and advantages of a franchise license, the franchisee pays an initial fee and an ongoing royalty. As a result, the franchisor receives a continuous supply of working capital to expand and develop the organization.

When you buy a franchise, you receive a business package which would otherwise take years to develop and refine — if ever. You also benefit from a strengthened ability to compete in the marketplace. Contributions collected from all the licensed outlets can finance major advertising campaigns that an independent operator could never afford. From these campaigns, you derive the image and marketing power of a giant. In addition, you obtain collective purchasing power, the envied status of self-management, and the know-how to avoid the pitfalls that doom most small-time operators.

But what about the franchisor? Why should a successful organization hand out its trade secrets and put you in business for yourself?

A franchisor's motives are not that different from yours. The franchisor gains the potential of building a business empire worth millions from an initial investment not greater than the top credit card limit extended today by banks and finance companies. He not only receives sizable royalty payments from the outlets' combined gross sales but also a steady stream of purchase orders as a wholesaler of supplies and equipment to the stores in the chain. Added to these obvious financial advantages of franchising, another powerful influence is at play in the franchise formula.

That factor is the franchisee's entrepreneurial spirit.

When franchisors recruit you to join their organizations, they are keenly interested in your personal ambition. As a rule, people who own their own businesses are more dedicated to success than are middle managers or department heads. That dedication translates into greater customer satisfaction and increased productivity. Franchising works for franchisors not just because it works for you, but because you also work for *it*.

But that wasn't always the case. Consider the story of Mary D., who wanted to transform her hobby — aerobic exercising — into a small business of her own.

The idea first came to her when she saw an ad for a "franchise opportunity" in the back of a health magazine. The words "huge profits" were draped across the top of the ad in big, bold print, and a stream of dollar bills descended along both sides. She called the phone number at the bottom and talked to the "franchisor" in person. The suave, articulate salesman convinced her to mail a check for $3,000 to purchase an "opening inventory" of exercise equipment.

Three weeks later, a delivery agent dropped several boxes of unassembled parts in her driveway. There were no assembly instructions, no sales training manuals, no business guides. She dialed the number in the ad to discover the "franchisor's" phone had been disconnected.

Overnight, Mary — and hundreds of other aerobics enthusiasts — were $3,000 poorer, with nothing but a garage full of useless parts to show for their investments.

The Regulatory Atmosphere

Not long ago, buying a franchise in itself was a risky venture. Practically anyone with an idea for sale, whether proved or not, could sell so-called "franchises" to eager, unsuspecting buyers. Many of those buyers ended up with little more than empty pockets and broken dreams.

Under today's complex regulations, franchisors must comply with a long list of disclosures and requirements. When the Federal Trade Commission introduced extensive franchise reform in 1980, more than half of the self-styled "franchisors" then in business disappeared almost overnight. The FTC rule is based on the 1971 California Franchise Investment Protection Law, which in turn was adapted from a paper created by a convention of Midwestern securities commissioners.

The first of the "full and accurate disclosure" laws governing franchise opportunities was passed by the California legislature in 1971. Since that time, fifteen other states have passed similar laws to regulate franchising. Franchisors who offer or sell franchises in these states must comply with a standardized format for disclosing information to prospective franchisees. A similar requirement is now enforced by the Federal Trade Commission for all franchisors — and would-be franchisors — operating in the U.S.

This disclosure format is called the Uniform Franchise Offering Circular, or UFOC. The UFOC is a document designed to inform potential franchisees about the background of those offering the franchise and the mutual obligations created by the franchise contract. In some states, this information must be filed with an agency responsible for monitoring franchises. A state regulator may have to approve the offering before it can be promoted to prospective franchise buyers.

The FTC requires franchisors in every state to provide a UFOC to prospective franchisees before the contract can be signed or any payment can be made. *If a franchise salesman asks a prospect to pay a deposit before the prescribed time period has elapsed* — and most assuredly, there are some who do — *it may be in violation of state or federal law.*

In most states with specific franchise laws, franchisors must also comply with the opinions of state-employed regulators. Such authorities have almost unlimited power over who may (and may not) do business in their states.

Even in unregulated states, a franchisor must follow the FTC's rules for full and accurate disclosure in the form of a UFOC prospectus. A potential buyer may not be coerced, persuaded, or tricked into signing until all the facts have been disclosed and clarified.

Rules and regulations are but one aspect of a modern franchise. In the remaining chapters, we will examine the psychological, ethical, sociological, legal, and financial forces that make franchising work, while exploring the subtle, sometimes volatile, chemistry that governs the franchise formula.

Chapter Two

To Franchise or Not to Franchise

A Self-Evaluation

Franchising is a bold and exhilarating adventure involving numerous decisions, both rational and emotional. You must recognize from the beginning that the decision to franchise is not an entirely intellectual consideration. There is an emotional side to every important decision, particularly one that will so profoundly affect your life, career, and well-being. Yet, it's important to balance that emotional part against the purely rational aspects of where you are now, where you want to be in the future, and how you are going to get there.

Listen to your brain, but give your heart equal time. No matter how logical a specific franchise choice might seem at the outset, unless you truly love the work involved, your commitment to success will be something less than total. And in the franchise game, nothing less than total commitment will do. In any industry, field, or trade, the perfect franchise will ultimately be the one that suits your personality as snugly as it fits your desires, abilities, and pocketbook.

Is franchising right for you? And, conversely, are you right for franchising? Despite its track record of creating successful small business owners, a franchise is not the perfect method of entrepreneurship

17

for everybody. On the opposite side of that coin, not everyone who wants to buy a franchise would make a good franchisee.

Before you leap into this adventure, devote some serious thought and time to self-evaluation. Exactly why should you consider franchising, rather than simply making a go of it on your own? Maybe you belong to the twenty percent of independent business owners who succeed on their own. Then again, your personality, aptitudes, and skills may be more like those of America's 700,000 franchise owners.

When you buy a franchise, you will have to sacrifice some measure of your entrepreneurial independence. Your franchisor will call many of the shots. Can you live with the obligations and restrictions of a franchise agreement?

A franchisor supplies training and guidance, but also a jolting array of mandatory policies and procedures. And yet, as a franchisee, you are an independent business owner, accountable for your business' success or failure. Are you willing to shoulder this burden?

A good place to start your self-evaluation is to compare yourself to the successful small business operators who have already made the franchise decision.

Who Buys Franchises?

The traits of successful franchisees were the subject of a three-year study by The Development Group, a consulting firm that works with franchise organizations. The consultants created a questionnaire designed to elicit personal information about those who apply for franchises. This questionnaire became part of the franchise application sent out by The Development Group's client firms during the study period.

The consultants studied the questionnaires of candidates who eventually became franchisees and compiled the table in Figure 2-1.

Figure 2-1

Sex	Male	87%
	Female	13
Education	College graduate	43
	High school	54

Marital Status	Single	34
	Married	66
Income	Less than $15,000	20
	$15,000 to $25,000	33
	$25,000 to $35,000	30
	More than $35,000	17
Previous	Less than 1 year	15
Managerial	1 to 5 years	75
Experience	5 years or more	10
Previously	Never	32
Owned a	Within last 5 years	49
Business	Within last 10 years	19
Reasons for	Self-management	73
Purchasing a	Financial independence	69
Franchise	Career advancement	53
	New skills/training	49
	Long-term investment	32
Sources	Financial publications	46
Consulted	Newspaper classified ads	36
Prior to	Trade journals	15
the Purchase	Consumer magazines	2
	Radio/TV	1

This study points out some interesting phenomena. The first reason a management-caliber American buys a franchise is the desire to be his own boss. Above all, most seek an opportunity for self-management and self-expression. Some may be frustrated with their current job and are on the lookout for independence. Or maybe it has always been their dream to run a successful business of their own.

Many franchisees actually sacrifice a portion of their earnings potential as wage earners for the opportunity to own their own businesses. Some of the franchise buyers in the three-year study had good incomes before setting out on their own, yet decided on franchise opportunities which they knew would not earn them as good a living as did their former occupations.

The owner of a small printing shop franchise said that when he was a regional sales manager for a book publisher he made twice what he does now as a franchisee. Yet, in his own words, he'd "never trade" his franchise for his old job — "not in a million years." In short, for most franchisees the psychological rewards take precedence over the financial.

You might think: Well, who wouldn't want to be his own boss? You may be surprised to find that many people would rather not have the headaches that come with the territory. Every platoon has only one commanding officer but many rank-and-file soldiers who would rather follow orders than formulate them. The franchisee is better-suited to be their leader, and he is neither a "private" nor a "general," but something closer to a "captain": capable of devising orders of his own, but reliant on the broad objectives and general guidance of a superior.

As you might guess, the second reason people buy franchises is the quest for financial growth, and ultimately riches. Many franchises are purchased strictly for investment purposes, like a diamond or security is bought for its speculative value. In fact, according to Department of Commerce statistics, about fifteen percent of America's franchises have "absentee" owners — people who buy a franchise for its investment value but hire others to manage the business.

But let's face it: everyone who goes into business for himself is pursuing a dream of financial independence and security. Those prone to buying franchises expect more from life than the seeming drudgery of a wage-earning career. They have a high level of ambition and an irrepressible belief that the rewards outweigh the risks. So, although money may not be the number one consideration in the minds of America's franchise owners, it's still high on the list.

The third reason for buying a franchise is the desire to be a winner. Most of us have a longing for a positive self-image and self-esteem. Franchisees enjoy the identity of success and, through their national tie-in, the industry dominance that accompanies the business. One owner of a restaurant franchise said he gladly paid an "exorbitant" franchise fee because the franchising company was "dripping with success." Many people buy franchises in the hope that some of their franchisor's successful image rubs off on their small businesses.

The fourth reason to buy a franchise is the most compelling one — to obtain training and guidance from an experienced insider. Franchisees are more likely than other entrepreneurs to recognize their own limitations. They know it takes a broad range of insights and skills to develop a successful business. After all, who among us is a competent chief executive and industry expert, as well as a master advertising director, skilled financial officer, and experienced personnel director?

Franchise buyers seek know-how and support in the broader aspects of running a business, especially advertising, accounting, and industry practices. The owner of three hairstyling franchises reported that he wanted "a big head start — no pun intended." Asked why he bought his SuperCuts franchises rather than simply open his own branch outlets, the excited entrepreneur responded: "I planned to open these parlors anyway.With a franchise, I have at least a three-year head start."

Lastly, people decide to buy franchises because they perceive the business to be an asset of lasting value. They believe the franchise has more permanence than other businesses, perhaps because a franchise agreement has a defined long term. Most independent enterprises are lucky to survive five years. In contrast, the average franchise agreement has a term of ten years, and is almost always renewable.

If you possess all of these motivating influences, then you *are* a prime candidate to buy or start a franchise. But to be really certain, you need to evaluate your mental, physical, and financial preparedness for the challenging task ahead.

Foster's Five Fs

In the food service industry — the largest segment of the franchise economy — there is a well-known standard for success called "Warfel's Five Gs" (Good food, Good service, Good prices, Good location, and Good management). Here's my own standard for success in franchising — one which shall go down in franchising history as "Foster's Five Fs":

1. Foresight
2. Flexibility
3. Fitness
4. Financing
5. Franchiseability

Ask yourself if you possess all — not just some — of these essential traits.

1. Foresight

Do you have a dream of owning your own business and being your own boss? Do you organize and plan for the future, or merely take things as they come?

2. Flexibility

Do you accept change readily and willingly? Do you adapt well to new people in your environment?

3. Fitness

Can you handle the stress that occurs with starting your own business? Are you in excellent health, both physically and mentally?

4. Financing

How do you propose to finance your business? Can you handle the moderate risk of failure? Will you need financial assistance, and, if so, where will you find it?

5. Franchiseability

Are you "franchiseable"? Are you willing to give up at least a portion of your independence in return for the benefits of a franchise organization? Do you have the leadership abilities and "people skills" it takes to succeed?

Here are some aids to help you assess the "Five Fs" in yourself.

Mental Preparedness: A Self-Test

Your mental preparedness involves more than a desire to be your own boss, or the willingness to shoulder responsibility. It also involves some more elusive traits, such as your level of self-confidence, your individual resourcefulness, and your overall attitude about people.

The following test may help you sort out your mental preparedness for franchising. Answer each question as frankly as possible (you can cheat only yourself). Each possible answer has an assigned point value, which is listed in the scoring table at the end. To determine your score, add up the point values of all the answers you selected. Then read the interpretation that corresponds to your total score.

Are You Mentally Prepared for Franchising?

1. True or False: Bosses have more headaches than their employees.
   (a) True
   (b) False

2. True or False: Employees are more passive than their bosses.
   (a) True
   (b) False

3. Is your work the main topic of conversation at the dinner table?
   (a) Often
   (b) Occasionally
   (c) Never

4. Are you upset when your work is performed well, and nobody notices?
   (a) Very
   (b) Somewhat
   (c) Not in the least

5. Do you do more work in less time than other people, or do more than your share?
   (a) Yes
   (b) No

6. Do you ever feel that you could do your boss's job better than he or she?
   (a) Often
   (b) Occasionally
   (c) Never

7. How would you characterize your work habits?
   (a) Meticulously organized
   (b) Generally quite organized
   (c) Sloppy, but who has the time?

8. Would you call yourself a "perfectionist?"
   (a) Yes
   (b) No

9. When you are solving a problem, or carrying out a job, how do you go about handling it?
   (a) I forge ahead without stopping until the problem is solved, or the job is finished.
   (b) I dedicate myself to the task when things are going smoothly, but know when to stop if the going gets too rough.
   (c) I have too many problems to solve, or too many jobs to do, to do any of them the way I think they should be done.

10. How willing are you to stake your savings on a business of your own?
    (a) Totally willing
    (b) Somewhat willing
    (c) Not willing

11. How long does it take you to adapt to a new boss, new employees, or new co-workers?
    (a) I readily accept new people and changing conditions in my work environment.
    (b) It takes a while, but eventually I accept change.
    (c) I have difficulty accepting new people and changing working conditions.

12. How would you describe your attitude about people in general?
    (a) I enjoy working with people, and they seem to enjoy working with me.
    (b) I get along with most people, and have relatively few enemies.
    (c) There are more important things in life than pleasing other people.

13. Do you enjoy working on a project by yourself?
    (a) I prefer having total responsibility for a project.
    (b) I like tackling projects alone, but with some advice and assistance from others.
    (c) I would rather work on a project as a member of a team, given clear and specific instructions.

14. How would you react if you started a business and it failed?

    (a) I would learn from my mistakes, and start over from scratch.

    (b) It would set me back temporarily, but I'd eventually recover.

    (c) I'm not a gambler; I never make a move if there's a risk of failure.

15. How do you feel about hard work?

    (a) I'd rather supervise hard work than take it on myself.

    (b) I'm not allergic to hard work, but I'd just as soon avoid it, if possible.

    (c) I enjoy my work, and believe that worthwhile results can only be achieved through serious effort.

16. How much experience have you had as a manager, supervisor, teacher, or trainer?

    (a) Five years or more

    (b) From one to five years

    (c) Less than a year

    (d) None

17. Have you ever owned a business before?

    (a) Yes

    (b) No

18. Do you feel you need more income to achieve your personal goals?

    (a) Yes

    (b) No

Scoring

    1. A-2 B-6
    2. A-6 B-2
    3. A-5 B-2 C-1
    4. A-5 B-2 C-1
    5. A-6 B-2
    6. A-5 B-2 C-1
    7. A-4 B-3 C-1
    8. A-5 B-3
    9. A-5 B-2 C-1
    10. A-5 B-2 C-1

11. A-5 B-2 C-1
12. A-5 B-2 C-1
13. A-3 B-4 C-1
14. A-4 B-3 C-1
15. A-1 B-2 C-5
16. A-3 B-2 C-1 D-0
17. A-5 B-3
18. A-6 B-2

Interpretation

78-89 A marriage made in franchise heaven!

You and franchising are a near-perfect match. It's time to wed your entrepreneurial spirit with a franchisor's training, guidance, and collective benefits. You have the same blend of self-confidence, commitment, flexibility, and drive that characterize most of America's 700,000 franchise owners.

65-77 A possible match.

Franchising may be right for you. You have many of the attributes that typify people who own franchises. But be careful to select a franchise backed by a well-established franchisor with a strong track record. Let your decision be guided by the franchisor's ability to fill the gaps in your own aptitudes and skills.

29-64 Outside chance.

Your level of ambition, confidence, and flexibility is different from that of most of those who bought franchises in the past. But that doesn't necessarily exclude you from the field. Ask yourself if you'll really be happier shouldering the responsibilities of owning your own business and risking your financial future. If, after finishing this book, you're still convinced that franchising is right for you, prepare yourself psychologically for the hard work, dedication, and effort that it will take to succeed.

Physical Preparedness

Aside from the obvious question of your present physical health, other factors are involved in your physical preparedness for a franchise. The most important is stress.

Major life changes make the body susceptible to physical illness. An individual experiencing a number of major life events in rapid succession has a higher risk of succumbing to a major illness than do other people. Changes such as the death of a family member, a divorce or separation, accidental injury, a job change or departure of a family member from the household all contribute to personal distress. Less profound changes affect us, too: vacation activities, changes in social activities and acquaintances, changes in living conditions, and changes in our financial situations.

The influence of job and work is an important factor in both mental and physical health. Getting a new job or leaving an old one, trouble with the boss or others in the company, deadlines, pressures, and problems provide a constant stream of stressors and anxieties.

The effect of life changes on physical health was the subject of an investigation by Adolf Meyer, a psychiatrist at Johns Hopkins Medical School. Dr. Meyer charted the social changes of his patients to see if there was a relationship between life events and illness. His charts revealed that his patients' illnesses generally coincided with major events in their personal lives.

This trend was confirmed by a behavioral scientist at Cornell University, Harold Wolff. In a study of 5,000 patients, he found that just before a major illness, there was a series of major life changes. The changes plotted by Dr. Meyer and Dr. Wolff included job-related stressors and social changes, ranging from getting a traffic ticket to changing jobs.

Leaving a job to start a new business is by itself a significant source of stress. Conducting a conscientious, sometimes arduous, franchise search compounds the potential effects on your physical well-being.

Take a few minutes to answer the questions in the following quiz, designed to gauge your physical preparedness for the effects of a strenuous franchise quest. Answer each question as truthfully as you can. See how your score corresponds to the situations and problems of those whom experts say run a high risk of becoming physically ill from stress.

27

Are You Physically Prepared to Handle the Stress of Starting a Franchise Business?

1. In the last month, have you had a serious disagreement with your boss?
   (a) Yes
   (b) No

2. Has your financial situation changed much, either for better or worse, in the last six months?
   (a) Yes
   (b) No

3. Were you fired from your last job?
   (a) Yes
   (b) No

4. Did you start your present job within the last six months?
   (a) Yes
   (b) No

5. Have you changed your working hours in the last ninety days?
   (a) Yes
   (b) No

6. Do you go to bed either earlier or later than you used to six months ago?
   (a) Yes
   (b) No

7. Have you changed jobs or been given new or different responsibilities in the last six months?
   (a) Yes
   (b) No

8. Has your spouse had a change in his or her job situation in the last six months? If not married, choose (b).
   (a) Yes
   (b) No

9. Do you do more work or less work than other people in the company with similar responsibilities?
   (a) More
   (b) Less
   (c) About the same

10. If you went to a party, would most of the people there be:
    (a) people you know because of your job
    (b) people you know outside of your job

11. Are you anticipating a vacation at some time in the next three months?
    (a) Yes
    (b) No

12. Has any member of your immediate family been taken seriously ill or been seriously injured in the last six months?
    (a) Yes
    (b) No

13. Have you taken out a bank loan or a mortgage in the last three months?
    (a) Yes
    (b) No

14. Do you have mostly different friends now than before you went to work?
    (a) Yes
    (b) No

15. Have you experienced any sexual difficulties in the last three months?
    (a) Yes
    (b) No

16. Have you disagreed with your spouse over any financial or household matters in the last three months? If not married, choose (b).
    (a) Yes
    (b) No

17. Do you have more than one alcoholic drink per day?
    (a) Often
    (b) Sometimes
    (c) Never

18. Do you have a doctor's prescription for a tranquilizer, sedative, or sleeping pill?
    (a) Yes
    (b) No

Scoring

  1. A-5 B-1
  2. A-5 B-1
  3. A-5 B-1
  4. A-5 B-1
  5. A-5 B-1
  6. A-5 B-1
  7. A-5 B-1
  8. A-5 B-1
  9. A-5 B-3 C-1
10. A-5 B-1
11. A-5 B-1
12. A-5 B-1
13. A-5 B-1
14. A-5 B-1
15. A-5 B-1
16. A-5 B-1
17. A-5 B-3 C-1
18. A-5 B-1

Interpretation

61-90 Stress! You've got it.

Your franchise quest will be a challenging, sometimes strenuous, adventure. Prepare yourself to fight stress with a regular exercise program, a nutritious diet, and some planned relaxation time. Take a short vacation before you start.

35-60 Marginal stress.

You're not a walking time bomb, but keep your guard up. Beware of health-threatening life events and changes as you set out in your own business. Work hard, but learn to relax.

24-34 No problem.

You're among a fortunate and exclusive group: you've barely been affected by stress. But, as you embark on your bold franchise quest, be on guard against pressures you may never have encountered before.

Financial Preparedness

Besides your mental and physical preparedness, you must also be prepared to handle the financial obligations of buying a franchise and sustaining the business until it becomes profitable.

Financial preparedness doesn't mean you have to have a large capital sum before you set out to find your perfect franchise opportunity. Many franchisors offer financial assistance. Moreover, numerous third parties, such as banks, savings and loan institutions, venture capital groups, and small business investment companies, may be able to help you finance the investment.

Still, you must be ready to accept the financial responsibility. A franchise minimizes your risk, but as in any business venture, there is a chance of failure. If your new business should fail despite your best efforts and those of your franchisor, would you be able to recover?

The degree of financial readiness that will be required depends on many factors, including the nature of the franchise you have in mind. After you have identified one or more franchises as potential investments, refer to the guidelines in Chapter Eight to determine exactly how much financing is required — and how much you can realistically expect to earn.

Before you begin your search, ask yourself the following questions:

- What is the maximum investment I am willing to undertake, including possible financial assistance from someone else?
- Am I willing to sign a personal guarantee for a business loan or other financial assistance?
- What is the type and amount of collateral I have available to back a loan request?
- If I don't have enough collateral, am I willing to give up a share of ownership in the business to a partner or investor?
- Will I have to focus my search exclusively on franchisors who offer financial assistance?
- What is the maximum investment I can handle without financial assistance?

31

Chapter Three

A Delicate Recipe

The Ingredients of a Franchise

$\mathbf{F}$or most people, the word "franchising" conjures up images of lightly warmed cheeseburgers or crispy fried chicken legs. In reality, franchises sell a huge variety of products, from hamburgers to computers. And while the recipe for a burger may be simple, the recipe for franchising success befits a culinary masterpiece: a delicate blend of several ingredients requiring balance, care, and attention to detail. The results depend on precise measurement and the exercise of patience. The relationships among the ingredients are often volatile, but their combined potency far outmeasures the sum of their parts.

A good recipe in the hands of a competent chef should produce the same results time after time. Similarly, a good franchise is a near-clone of all the other franchises in a franchisor's network.

A modern franchise has three main ingredients:

- an *identity*, based on a trade name protected for exclusive use by the franchise holders;
- an *operating system*, or business format, ready to be transferred to the fee-paying franchisee;
- a *continuous financial relationship*, usually a lump sum paid in advance, plus an ongoing royalty based on an established percentage of gross revenues.

33

The franchisee is an independent business owner who contracts with the franchisor to obtain the right to put these ingredients to use. The franchisee provides nearly all the working capital to establish and develop the outlet. The franchisor supplies his idea, an established identity, a fine-tuned operating system, and, in many cases, the product.

Here's how the International Franchise Association defines franchising:

> A franchise is a continuing relationship between franchisor and franchisee in which the sum total of the franchisor's knowledge, image, success, manufacturing, and marketing techniques are supplied to the franchisee for a consideration.

Ideally, when you purchase a franchise, you are also purchasing a pre-packaged business. Although you own its every asset, your franchisor may have astrong voice in how you run your business. The cornerstone of the franchise is a contractual agreement which defines both the rights and the obligations of you and your franchisor.

Business-Format Franchising

Buying or selling a franchise based on a packaged business concept is called *business-format franchising*. This form of franchising accounts for more than ninety percent of the franchise operations in business today.

Let's take a closer look at the three essential ingredients in a business-format franchise.

• *A Valued Identity*

Foremost, a franchisor offers his good name in the industry. A successful identity is one of the hallmarks of the franchise offering; therefore the franchisor must be capable of substantiating its value.

Both you and your franchisor should be prepared to protect that identity against infringement by others. One of the things you are buying when you sign a franchise agreement is the right to use the franchisor's registered trademarks.

The worth of a franchise identity is also derived from the recognition, reputation, and goodwill of the franchise organization. People who invest in franchises are looking for a successful image. When you take on a franchise, your franchisor's identity, in effect, becomes *your* identity.

You may be John Smith or Jane Doe when you sign the franchise agreement, but when the sign outside your business lights up for the first time, you'll suddenly become Mr. Pizza Parlor . . . Ms. Computer Store . . . or Mr. and Mrs. Car Rental Agency.

● *A Finely Tuned Operating System*

One of the most important components of franchising is the ease with which the organization's systems and procedures can be transferred to a franchisee. When you buy a franchise, you are acquiring more than just a trade name: you are also obtaining a verifiable formula for success.

Some franchisors go so far as to provide a complete "turn-key" operation: when you graduate from franchise school, you receive the keys to a fully developed business. More commonly, a franchisor will equip you with blueprints, manuals, specifications, and training, relying on your initiative to get the business established.

The franchisor's "how-to" bible is the franchise operating manual. The manual covers everything from accounting procedures to employee supervision. It also documents standards and policies that all franchisees are expected to follow.

The franchisor loans the manual to the franchisee for the term of the franchise agreement. On expiration or termination of the franchise, he must return the book in its entirety. This requirement helps to maintain the aura of secrecy about the franchise system and the know-how it takes to run it. After all, if the formula wasn't secret, why would you pay good money to obtain it?

● *An Ongoing Financial Relationship*

In return for the franchisor's valued identity and finely tuned operating system, the franchisee pays a fee. The most common franchise fee consists of three parts: (1) an initial payment due on signing of the franchise agreement; (2) a continuous royalty, usually charged on the

35

gross revenues of the outlet; and (3) a royalty or contribution to a co-operative advertising fund.

It's common for a new or small franchise to have a relatively small fee. Conversely, the larger the network, the more you can expect to pay for the privilege of joining.

The Burger King franchise is a good example of that principle. When this famous hamburger chain first opened the gate to its franchise corral, the initial fee was as low as $300. Like thirsty cattle at the trough, entrepreneurs hastily bought up several hundred franchises in a span of two years. By the end of that period, the initial fee had swollen over hundred times to more than $30,000. Yet new franchisees gladly paid the inflated sum for the right to join the rapidly proliferating network.

Why is an established franchise more valuable than a new one? In the first place, the elder franchise statesman has a demonstrated track record. Moreover, the sheer number of participants maximizes such collective benefits as co-op advertising and volume purchasing.

Franchising by Any Other Name

When is a franchise not a franchise? And when is a "business opportunity" really a franchise offer? Often, many investments promoted as franchises do not incorporate all the essential ingredients. The term franchise implies backing, support, and a strong likelihood of success. Yet many so-called franchise offerings are little more than trade name licenses or highly priced sales territories. Do these offerings fall under franchise regulation?

The California Franchise Investment Protection Law, and similar laws in other states, consider an offering to be a franchise whenever the word "franchise" is used in promotion. But what about the carefully named "business opportunity" that seems to have the ingredients of a franchise but is promoted as an alternative?

A franchise doesn't have to be called a franchise in order to fall under the scope of the law. As a matter of fact, some state regulators spend the greater part of their time investigating franchise-like opportunities in order to identify unethical operators.

In regulated states such as California, New York, and Illinois, any business that sells the right to a trade name or business format and receives a payment for that right is a franchise, no matter what term the promoter may use. Be wary of any promoter who claims not to be a franchisor but offers you the right to use a trade name for a fee.

Most but not all of the franchises legally offered are business-format franchises. Others involve only a trade name, a sales territory, or both. But it is the full business-format franchise, combining the mainstays of an established identity and a protected territory with the benefits of industry training and refined operating systems, that inspired the franchise revolution of modern times.

But how was it, you might wonder, that this revolution ever took place?

The Franchisee's Edge

Most independently owned businesses are doomed from the day they open their doors. The owners of the twenty percent that actually manage to make it past the first critical five years spend much of that time experimenting with trial-and-error decisions, puzzling over the right path to survival. In contrast, a franchisee has a good idea where that path lies from the moment he graduates from his franchisor's training school.

As a franchise chain increases in size, its franchisees benefit from heightened exposure and a bigger advertising budget. But the franchise owner has another important edge over other entrepreneurs: American consumers tend to favor the franchise establishment.

The Security of Sameness

Sameness is a basic component in consumer consciousness. Few fears are more pronounced than the fear of the unknown, and nowhere is this principle more evident than in consumer buying behavior.

Who has not balked at turning into an unknown fast-food stand by the highway, or driven past an anonymous motel in quest of a recognizable name? Whose imagination has not conjured up nightmarish images of grease-encrusted grills, derelict washrooms, and unscrupulous cigar-puffing managers?

We Americans patronize the known establishment, in part, because we fear the unknown. A franchise is a known commodity. If you've had one "last honest pizza," you've had them all. But who knows what unsavory ingredients lurk beneath the cheesy surface of a "Bruno's Bar and Grill" pizza? If you've slept in one Holiday Inn, you have a pretty decent idea what it's like to sleep in any of them. But who knows whether the plumbing even works at the "Have-a-Ball Motel?"

Even if you've never patronized a particular franchise chain, you somehow trust an establishment simply because it's a franchise. You know its floors are likely to be clean, its employees groomed, and its plumbing in working order. You also have an idea of what prices it charges. You have no such assurances when you deal with a non-franchise establishment.

We expect a Big Mac to taste the same in downtown Manhattan as in Des Moines, Iowa — or Paris, France, for that matter. We expect a room at the Sheraton Inn in Seattle to have approximately the same decor as the one in Norman, Oklahoma. Whether we rent a Hertz car in Tijuana, Mexico or Detroit, Michigan, we expect it to run as well.

As you begin your search for an ideal franchise business, you probably will be startled by the dramatic variation in the level of image, refinement, and sophistication among franchise organizations. Some franchisors will seem aggressive, organized, and professional. Others will strike you as methodical, plodding, and rough-edged. Still others may come across as slick, rigid, or too anxious to close a deal.

Remember that the franchise decision has three aspects: rational, emotional, and financial. The following list will help you organize your thoughts, keep the franchise search in perspective, and refrain from making a costly mistake.

Evaluating the Ingredients of a Franchise

Franchise Identity

- Is the franchise trade name well known? If not, is it "catchy" or unique enough to justify buying a franchise?
- Is the name so similar to another business name or trade mark that it might cause confusion?

- Is anyone else already using the same or a similar name or trademark in your trading area? If so, can you obtain the right to use the name or trademark from the party already using it? How much will it cost?
- Is the image of the business conducive to your own personality and self-esteem?
- How do you feel about being known as the "owner" or "president" of this business?

Operating System

- Does the franchisor offer a training program? If so, how long is it? What topics does it cover?
- Will the franchisor help you select a site for the business?
- Does the franchisor provide a franchise operating manual? If so, what subjects are included?
  Grand Opening?
  Setting up books and records?
  Accounting and reports?
  Advertising and publicity?
  Purchasing and inventory?
  Marketing and sales?
  Daily operating procedures?
  Cleanliness and grooming?
  Employee policies and procedures?
  Technical information?
- Does the franchisor provide pre-designed signs, menus, fixtures, decorations, etc.? If not, will he help you procure them?
- Can the franchisor help you purchase equipment, supplies, or inventory at a discount? Is it really a discount?

Financial Relationship

- Is there an initial franchise fee?
- Does the fee vary from one location to another? If so, what is the amount of the fee for the location or territory you have in mind?
- Does the franchisor charge an ongoing franchise royalty? If so, what is the percentage?

- Is the royalty set for the entire term of the franchise, or can it be raised or lowered in the future?
- If the royalty is not set, what factors will the franchisor use to determine it?
- Does the franchisor charge a co-op advertising royalty in addition to the basic franchise royalty?
- Is the co-op advertising royalty set for the entire term of the franchise, or can it be raised or lowered in the future?

Chapter Four

The Price of Admission

Franchise Fees and Royalties

To you, a franchise represents a business opportunity. It consists of a valued name, a packaged format, industry training, and other considerations. To a franchisor, the franchise is his product. Like the products and services a franchisee sells in the marketplace, the franchise has a price.

In a capitalist economy, every product has at least two price components: cost and profit. For example, a grocer buys a loaf of bread from a bakery for fifty cents and resells it for a dollar. In addition to the fifty cents he paid to the bakery, the grocer has also incurred other costs in connection with the loaf — delivery, labeling, stocking, etc. Let's say this "overhead" amount is ten cents per loaf on the average. So the first sixty cents of the resale dollar covers the grocer's product costs. The remaining forty cents is profit.

Contrary to popular belief, the price of a franchise is not unlike the grocer's price for a loaf of bread. Many believe the initial fee paid by a franchisee is a source of profit for the franchisor. In reality, the initial fee represents the *cost component* of the franchise. It is from collective, ongoing royalty payments from franchisees that a franchisor hopes to derive profits.

To understand why this is so, you must imagine yourself in a franchisor's shoes. When a franchisor first sets out to offer franchises, he establishes a value for the initial fee, the royalty, and advertising fund contribution. The first issue he confronts is the initial fee.

The Initial Fee

When a franchisor and franchisee consummate an agreement, the franchisee typically pays an initial fee. It may surprise you to learn that franchisors don't sit around with their feet propped up on their desks, thinking: "Well, maybe I can get $10,000 . . . or who knows? Maybe $20,000." The initial franchise fee compensates the franchisor for the costs of recruiting, training, and assisting new franchisees. In fact, many of the states that individually regulate franchising require franchisors to disclose exactly how they calculated their initial fees.

Most initial fees take into consideration the following five factors:

- the value of the business, or its goodwill;
- the value of the trading area or territory;
- the cost of recruiting a single franchisee;
- the cost of training the franchisee;
- the cost of signs, ads, plans, or other aids.

To envision how these factors influence the franchise fee, let's continue to assume that, instead of a potential franchisee considering an investment, you are a franchisor seeking to sell franchise opportunities to others.

The Value of the Business

As you start out, you have no franchises sold or open. Consequently, to place a value on the franchise will require intelligent guessing. The newer the franchise and the fewer its outlets, the more minuscule its demonstrable value. Goodwill is perhaps the least tangible of all the variables.

By "goodwill," a business owner means the reputation of the business — its ability to attract either new or repeat customers. As such, goodwill is considered an asset of the business, because when the business is sold, its goodwill is transferred to the new owners.

However, in the franchise trade, the value of goodwill is usually perceived, not calculated. Thus, it nearly always equals franchisee demand. In other words, goodwill is never less valuable than the maximum amount anyone is willing to pay for it. For instance, how much more valuable is the right to own a restaurant named MacDonald's than the right to own one named Joe's? It's basically whatever people are willing to pay.

Nonetheless, there are some ways to place a fair price on goodwill. An investment broker often estimates goodwill at four to twelve percent of the market value of the business. He calculates the market value by multiplying the business's annual profits times two and a half. For example, a business that generates $100,000 per year in profits should theoretically be worth about $250,000. Figured at twelve percent, a high — but not necessarily unreasonable — rate, the value of goodwill would be about $30,000. At four percent — a more common yardstick — the value would be $10,000.

But with a new franchise, the business's value is usually hypothetical. Hence, demand almost always dictates the value. Based on the maximum price the seller can command, the same franchise may sell for different prices at different times or in different parts of the country. Bear in mind that in the case of an established franchise the seller may not be the franchisor, but rather a franchise broker or franchisee selling off his business.

As a general rule, the more outlets, the higher the initial fee. For example, a new franchisor might start out offering franchises with an initial fee of only a few hundred dollars. In some instances, he might grant some franchises without charging any initial fee, simply to get the ball rolling.

If you are considering a franchise which is just getting off the ground, you should expect a "sweetheart" deal; no matter how successful the franchisor's original business, he does not yet have a demonstrated track record in franchising. You are assuming a proportionately higher risk, and are justified in expecting some form of compensation or compromise.

The Fees and Royalties Checklist at the conclusion of this chapter includes some important questions about how a franchisor justifies the value of his franchises.

• *The Value of the Trading Area*

Besides the intangible value of the business's identity and goodwill, the initial fee often reflects the value of an exclusive territory or trading area. In this case, the franchisor bases part of the fee on marketing statistics and demographics to estimate the relative worth of a specific territory. He can either carve out franchise territories of equal worth, or vary the initial fee based on the relative worth of the territory.

We'll see how territories can be appraised later in this chapter.

• *The Costs of Recruiting, Training, and Sustaining*

The remaining factors reflected in the initial fee are much more tangible than goodwill or the potential market. For example, the cost of recruiting a franchisee can be estimated with a fair amount of accuracy. This amount includes costs attributable to advertising, lead processing, administration, and accounting. Similarly, the franchisee training program has an identifiable cost that must be integrated in the initial fee. In addition, the franchisor must recover costs of printing the franchise operating manual, reproducing architectural plans, assisting with site selection, signs, and any other assistance inherent in the franchise agreement.

For example, let's say that as a new franchisor you are planning to sell fifty franchises in the forthcoming fiscal year. If your advertising budget for the year is $100,000, it will cost you $2,000 to recruit each new franchisee. Let's say your operating budget includes $250,000 to run your franchise training school. You will thus incur training costs of $5,000 per franchisee. As you can see, you must already recover at least $7,000 per franchisee just to cover your costs. Add to that figure such costs as the franchise operating manual, site selection assistance, telephone and communications, etc., and it is not difficult to see why initial fees in excess of $10,000 are common.

In the case of a franchisor who has very few outlets open, again, you would expect the initial fee to be quite low — just enough to cover actual costs of recruiting, training, and putting you in business. With an established franchisor whose name is well known, you would expect a disproportionate value placed on goodwill and intangibles — but a value you might be willing to pay.

Following are some examples of initial fees in various trade categories, based on actual franchise advertisements:

Automotive
Budget Rent-a-Car	$15,000
Midas Muffler	10,000
Jiffy Lube	25,000
Goodyear Tire	none
Aamco Transmission	25,000

Business Services
VR Business Brokers	9,500
General Business Services	21,500
Snelling & Snelling	14,000
Postal Instant Press	40,000
Western Temporary	25,000

Food Service
Kentucky Fried Chicken	20,000
Wendy's	30,000
Taco Bell	35,000
Pizza Hut	15,000

Retailing
Computerland	25,000
Video Connection	none
7-Eleven Stores	12,500
Pier One Imports	16,400

Bear in mind that the initial fees above are the franchisors' reported minimum fees, so it would not be unusual to find one or more of these franchises offered at a higher price.

The Franchise Royalty

The franchise royalty, like the initial fee, should reflect the worth and maturity of the business. The first few franchises are usually offered at both a low fee and a low royalty. Few investors want to be a franchisor's first franchise operator. Conversely, a ground-floor franchisee often enjoys the most dramatic growth because he gets in for less money.

As more outlets begin to open, the initial fee and royalty are usually raised. For example, let's say you're a new franchisor about to enter the marketplace. To attract franchisees, you set the initial fee at $2,000 and the monthly royalty at 3.5 percent of gross revenues. At this appealing price, you rapidly sell six franchises, instantly increasing the actual and perceived value of the business. You raise the initial fee to $4,000 and the monthly royalty to five percent.

Now, that does not mean that your existing six franchisees have to pay more than they originally bargained for. You are obliged to honor their franchise agreements, but free to institute the new fees to all subsequent franchisees. (Both the initial fee and the royalty are required to be disclosed in the franchisor's offering circular, so any increase requires a new UFOC as well as an amendment to the application for franchise registration in individually regulated states, such as California, Illinois, or New York.)

Let's say you sell another twelve franchises at the higher price. The value of the franchise has increased still more, so you decide to raise the fee to $6,000 and the royalty to 7.5 percent. You now have six franchisees who paid you $2,000 each in initial fees and who continue to pay a royalty of 3.5 percent of gross monthly revenues. In addition, another twelve who paid $4,000 in initial fees are paying out five percent of their gross incomes. But anyone else who buys a franchise will have to pay the new amount — $6,000 plus 7.5 percent in royalties.

As you can see from this illustration, high fees generally indicate an advanced level of maturity in a franchise organization. As you evaluate franchise opportunities, be sure to compare a franchisor's fees with others in the same field. Contrast the size, experience, and recognition of the franchisor's organization with the others. Ask yourself: are the fees justifiable in relation to competition? Do they accurately reflect the franchisor's number of years in the industry? Does the franchisor have more outlets than franchisors who command lower fees?

Royalties vary significantly from one franchise to another. A Budget car rental franchisee pays 7.5 percent of gross monthly sales to the franchisor. A Kentucky Fried Chicken restaurant pays just four percent. The owner of a Baskin-Robbins ice cream parlor pays no royalty at all; however, he purchases equipment, supplies, and ice cream from his franchisor.

The Co-op Advertising Royalty

Besides the initial fee and monthly royalty, most franchisors also require franchisees to pay a monthly ad royalty. The outlet contributes a small percentage of its gross income into a co-op fund. Monies accruing in this ad fund are pooled to finance national and regional advertising campaigns for the benefit of all franchisees.

The co-op ad fund benefits the individual franchise owner by financing major advertising programs that would otherwise be unaffordable. The franchisor benefits from increased exposure of the trade name and business, thus increasing the value of the franchise and the flow of royalty dollars.

You should note that not all franchisors have a co-op ad fund. Many franchise systems do quite well without a centralized advertising program by requiring franchisees to conduct and pay for their own advertising. Unhappily, this practice often leads to a loss of control over image. It also tends to alienate franchisees because of the deterioration of standards — the loss of the security of sameness that catalyzes the franchise formula.

Ad royalties range from a fraction of one percent to several percentage points. Burger King restaurants pay four percent of gross revenues into their ad pool. A Holiday Inn pays two percent. An Athletic Annex footwear store pays only one half of one percent.

Figure 4-1 illustrates the principle of the ascending franchise fee. The initial fee and the franchise royalty are the most likely to increase as a franchise organization proliferates, while the co-op advertising royalty usually remains constant. After all, the ad fund benefits every franchisee equally.

Figure 4-1 An example of an ascending franchise fee

	Outlets 1-29	Outlets 30-77	Outlets 78 +
Fee	$20,000	25,000	30,000
Royalty	5%	6.25	7.5
Ad Fund	1%	1	1

When prospective franchise buyers research the field, they often focus their attention on franchise fees and royalties, overlooking a far more meaningful price component: the total initial investment.

The Initial Investment

On the surface, a franchise with an initial fee of $10,000 might seem like a bargain compared to one offered at $35,000. But a more meaningful comparison is one which contrasts the total initial investments: How much will it cost to start each type of business above and beyond the initial fee?

The Uniform Franchise Offering Circular (UFOC), which all franchisors are required to prepare, must indicate the franchisee's total initial investment. The investment breakdown includes the initial fee, plus the cost of procuring and developing a site. It must show the cost of all equipment, leases, fixtures, and inventory required to operate the business. It may also include working capital for out-of-pocket expenses during the startup period, i.e., before the business becomes profitable. However, franchisors are not specifically required to estimate working capital requirements.

Figure 4-2 shows an example of a franchisor's disclosure of a franchisee's estimated initial investment for a typical retail outlet. In Chapter Ten, we'll take a closer look at the actual costs of getting into a franchise business.

Figure 4-2 An example of a franchisee's initial investment breakdown

Initial Fee	$20,000
Leases	4,000
Improvements	5,000
Equipment/Fixtures	5,000
Inventory	20,000
Filing/Legal	500
Insurance	500
Working Capital	10,000
Total Initial Investment	65,000

The Franchise Organization

To some extent, how the franchise system is organized is dictated by the way initial fees and royalties are paid. For instance, when you buy a franchise, you may not be dealing with the franchisor, but rather with a sub-franchisor or franchise broker. If you become the franchisee of a sub-franchisor, you may end up paying royalties not to the original franchisor, but to the person who sold you the franchise. That party, in turn, pays royalties to someone else, e.g., the franchisor or another sub-franchisor.

The system of organization in a franchise network is referred to as the "ultrastructure." The *satellite system* is the simplest form of ultrastructure. Like moons revolving around a planet, the franchisee-owned "satellites" operate independently, but under the global influence of the franchisor. Retail stores like Little Professor Book Centers, Computerland, and Taylor Rentals are representative of satellite franchises.

In this type of organization, each outlet is directly accountable to the franchisor. There are no sub-franchisors or marketing levels between the franchisee and the franchisor. You pay the initial fee and all ongoing royalties directly to your franchisor.

When you buy a franchise in a satellite system, you may also obtain a protected territory. On the premise that restraining a franchisee within predefined boundaries is anti-competitive, the courts generally frown on exclusive franchise territories. However, a franchisor *can* offer a "protected" territory in which he promises not to sell another franchise. He may not, on the other hand, attempt to restrain a franchisee from selling to customers outside his protected territory.

For example, let's say you purchase a franchise to sell real estate in a particular geographical area. Your franchisor can grant you a "protected territory," which means he will refrain from establishing other franchises or selling real estate services in competition with your franchise. But he is legally prohibited from denying you access to customers outside your territory. So, even though your franchise may have predefined geographical boundaries, you are free to cultivate business anywhere you choose.

By granting a territory, and agreeing not to compete with you within that territory, a franchisor instantly creates value. What is a franchise territory worth? The answer to that question depends, among other things, on the nature of the business, the size of the territory, and local economic conditions.

Evaluating a Franchise Territory

The tables in Figures 4-3 through 4-7 rank various franchise industries by major market. These tables were compiled by The Development Group to help franchisors determine the relative value of different geographical territories. The consultants weighed the overall economic strength of each market and the amount of money spent by businesses on advertising.

You can use these tables yourself as a general guide to what a franchise territory should be worth in different areas. Each table shows a rank, the name of the market, and a "relative value."

For example, in Figure 4-3, the Los Angeles market is ranked number one among top retail markets, with a relative value of 32.28. In contrast, in the same table, Phoenix is ranked seventeenth, with a relative value of 8.04 — or about one fourth the relative value of Los Angeles. Thus, a franchise territory which includes Los Angeles should be worth about four times as much as one which includes Phoenix.

Assume you are considering a franchise in Los Angeles. Your franchisor plans to sell five franchises in that city for an initial fee of $10,000 each. Hence, the franchisor's total valuation for the market is $50,000. If you were to buy a franchise in Phoenix from the same franchisor, you should expect the initial fee to be in the neighborhood of $12,500 (one fourth the total value of the Los Angeles one). If the franchisor planned on selling two franchises in Phoenix, each should be priced at about half, or roughly $6,250.

Unfortunately, not all franchisors use marketing statistics to evaluate the relative worth of franchise territories. Moreover, bear in mind that the value of the market or territory is only one factor in the initial franchise fee. No matter what the market, the franchisor must be able to recoup from the initial fee the costs of recruiting, training, and assisting new franchisees.

Figure 4-3

Top Retail Markets

Rank	Market	Relative Value
1	Los Angeles	32.28
2	Chicago	31.92
3	New York	31.44
4	Philadelphia	19.20
5	Detroit	17.16
6	Boston	15.84
7	San Francisco	14.28
8	Houston	14.16
9	Washington, DC	13.32
10	Dallas	12.24
11	Nassau, NY	11.28
12	St. Louis	9.60
13	San Diego	9.24
14	Minneapolis	9.12
15	Pittsburgh	8.88
16	Anaheim, CA	8.88
17	Phoenix	8.60
18	Cleveland	8.04
19	Atlanta	8.04
20	Newark	7.92
21	Miami	7.32
22	Baltimore	7.20
23	Seattle	7.08
24	Denver	6.60
25	Tampa	6.48
26	Kansas City	6.36
27	Milwaukee	6.12
28	Cincinatti	5.64
29	San Jose, CA	5.52
30	Indianapolis	5.40
31	Ft. Lauderdale	5.40
32	Riverside, CA	5.40
33	Columbus, OH	5.40
34	New Orleans	4.68

Figure 4-3 continued

Top Retail Markets

Rank	Market	Relative Value
35	Portland	4.56
36	Buffalo	4.32
37	Hartford, CT	4.19
38	Sacramento, CA	3.70
39	Birmingham	3.84
40	San Antonio	3.84
41	Memphis	3.79
42	Oklahoma City	3.74
43	Louisville	3.73
44	Bridgeport, CT	3.55
45	Rochester, NY	3.55
46	Nashville	3.54
47	Salt Lake City	3.48
48	Dayton, OH	3.40
49	Orlando	3.31
50	Providence, RI	3.30

Figure 4-4

Top Food and Beverage Markets

Rank	Market	Relative Value
1	Los Angeles	34.56
2	New York	32.16
3	Chicago	30.84
4	San Francisco	16.00
5	Philadelphia	15.85
6	Boston	15.43
7	Detroit	14.81
8	Washington, DC	13.27
9	Houston	11.87
10	Dallas	11.11
11	Anaheim, CA	9.85

Figure 4-4 continued

Top Food and Beverage Markets

Rank	Market	Relative Value
12	Minneapolis	8.74
13	Atlanta	8.57
14	Nassau, NY	8.50
15	St. Louis	7.91
16	Miami	7.69
17	Cleveland	7.32
18	Baltimore	7.31
19	San Diego	7.25
20	Seattle	7.14
21	Pittsburgh	6.88
22	Phoenix	6.73
23	Newark	6.34
24	Tampa	6.11
25	Milwaukee	6.02
26	Cincinatti	5.57
27	Denver	5.54
28	Kansas City	5.45
29	Ft. Lauderdale	5.21
30	Indianapolis	5.11
31	Riverside, CA	4.91
32	Columbus, OH	4.85
33	New Orleans	4.82
34	San Jose, CA	4.79
35	Honolulu	4.66
36	Portland	4.39
37	Buffalo	4.38
38	San Antonio	4.00
39	Hartford, CT	3.89
40	Dayton, OH	3.46
41	Toledo	3.32
42	Orlando	3.31
43	Salt Lake City	3.28
44	Oklahoma City	3.17
45	Providence, RI	3.13
46	Sacramento, CA	3.08

Figure 4-4 continued

Top Food and Beverage Markets

Rank	Market	Relative Value
47	Birmingham	2.89
48	Louisville	2.87
49	Nashville	2.86
50	Bridgeport, CT	2.78

Figure 4-5

Top Appliance and Electronics Markets

Rank	Market	Relative Value
1	New York	34.56
2	Chicago	32.16
3	Los Angeles	30.84
4	San Francisco	16.00
5	Philadelphia	15.85
6	Washington, DC	15.43
7	Boston	14.81
8	Houston	13.27
9	Dallas	11.87
10	Nassau, NY	11.11
11	Minneapolis	9.85
12	St. Louis	8.74
13	Anaheim, CA	8.57
14	Atlanta	8.50
15	Pittsburgh	7.91
16	Detroit	7.83
17	Phoenix	7.69
18	San Diego	7.32
19	Miami	7.31
20	Denver	7.25
21	Cleveland	7.14
22	Tampa	6.88
23	Baltimore	6.73

Figure 4-5 continued

Top Appliance and Electronics Markets

Rank	Market	Relative Value
24	Newark	6.34
25	Milwaukee	6.11
26	Kansas City	6.02
27	San Jose, CA	5.57
28	Terre Haute, IN	5.54
29	Seattle	5.45
30	Columbus, OH	5.21
31	Cincinatti	5.11
32	Indianapolis	4.91
33	Riverside, CA	4.85
34	Ft. Lauderdale	4.82
35	Portland	4.79
36	Sacramento, CA	4.66
37	New Orleans	4.39
38	San Antonio	4.38
39	Buffalo	4.00
40	Dayton, OH	3.89
41	Oklahoma City	3.46
42	Memphis	3.32
43	York, PA	3.31
44	Orlando	3.28
45	Honolulu	3.17
46	Hartford, CT	3.13
47	Toledo	3.08
48	Birmingham	2.89
49	Louisville	2.87
50	Nashville	2.86

Figure 4-6

Top Health-Services Markets

Rank	Market	Relative Value
1	Los Angeles	32.00
2	New York	30.35
3	Chicago	23.90
4	Washington, DC	19.85
5	Philadelphia	18.95
6	Houston	17.00
7	San Francisco	15.65
8	Dallas	14.85
9	Boston	12.70
10	St. Louis	11.80
11	Cleveland	9.35
12	Detroit	8.30
13	Nassau, NY	8.10
14	Pittsburgh	7.95
15	Baltimore	7.75
16	San Diego	7.50
17	Anaheim, CA	7.45
18	Tampa	6.85
19	Seattle	6.80
20	Phoenix	6.60
21	Kansas City	6.30
22	Newark	6.20
23	Atlanta	6.15
24	Minneapolis	6.10
25	Miami	5.55
26	Cincinnati	5.31
27	New Orleans	4.68
28	Denver	4.64
29	Indianapolis	4.55
30	San Jose, CA	4.47
31	Milwaukee	4.42
32	Buffalo	4.37
33	Columbus, OH	4.14
34	Honolulu	4.11

Figure 4-6 continued

Top Health-Services Markets

Rank	Market	Relative Value
35	Hartford, CT	3.83
36	Louisville	3.81
37	Riverside, CA	3.78
38	Norfolk, VA	3.75
39	Oklahoma City	3.62
40	Birmingham	3.56
41	Rochester, NY	3.50
42	Richmond	3.41
43	Salt Lake City	3.38
44	Ft. Lauderdale	3.18
45	Portland	3.14
46	Tulsa	3.10
47	Memphis	3.08
48	Omaha	3.05
49	Gary, IN	2.99
50	Nashville	2.98

Figure 4-7

Top Apparel and Soft Goods Markets

Rank	Market	Relative Value
1	New York	34.56
2	Chicago	32.16
3	Los Angeles	30.84
4	San Francisco	16.00
5	Philadelphia	15.85
6	Boston	15.43
7	Washington, DC	14.81
8	Houston	13.27
9	Dallas	11.87
10	Nassau, NY	11.11
11	Detroit	10.72
12	Newark	9.85

Figure 4-7 continued

Top Apparel and Soft Goods Markets

Rank	Market	Relative Value
13	Miami	8.74
14	Pittsburgh	8.57
15	Minneapolis	8.50
16	Anaheim, CA	7.91
17	Seattle	7.83
18	St. Louis	7.69
19	Baltimore	7.32
20	Cleveland	7.31
21	New Orleans	7.25
22	Atlanta	7.14
23	San Jose, CA	6.88
24	Denver	6.73
25	San Diego	6.34
26	Kansas City	6.11
27	Buffalo	6.02
28	Riverside, CA	5.57
29	Ft. Lauderdale	5.54
30	Jersey City	5.45
31	Hartford, CT	5.21
32	Birmingham	5.11
33	Oklahoma City	4.91
34	Milwaukee	4.85
35	Tampa	4.82
36	Columbus, OH	4.79
37	Nashville	4.66
38	Indianapolis	4.39
39	New Haven, CT	4.38
40	Paterson, NJ	4.00
41	Tulsa	3.89
42	Memphis	3.46
43	Portland	3.32
44	Bridgeport, CT	3.31
45	Sacramento, CA	3.28
46	Phoenix	3.17
47	Cincinnati	3.13

Figure 4-7 continued

Top Apparel and Soft Goods Markets

Rank	Market	Relative Value
48	Greensboro, NC	3.08
49	Norfolk, VA	2.89
50	San Antonio	2.87

Area Franchising

An alternative (or in some cases, an adjunct) to satellite franchising is *area franchising*. In this strategy, the franchisor licenses a "master" area franchisee in a large marketing area — for instance, an entire state or region. The area franchisee in turn sub-franchises within the granted territory. If you were the franchisor, you could grant the area franchisee the right to open as many outlets as the territory can sustain, or you could limit him to a specified number.

Century 21 Real Estate is a good example of area franchising. A master franchisee, who originally purchases area rights to a large geographical territory, sub-franchises many Century 21 offices. The individual outlets function as satellites of the area franchisee. The franchisor, in turn, controls the area franchisees, who take care of the satellite stores. Each satellite pays fees and royalties to the area franchisee, who then pays royalties to the franchisor.

To maintain control over the franchises in the various levels and sublevels of the organization, the franchisor sends out "area controllers." But the area franchisee shoulders the burden of recruiting and, in some cases, training new franchisees.

By area franchising, a franchisor realizes the greatest short-term cash flow at the least initial overhead. Consider a franchisor planning to sell three hundred franchises over one year. His recruiting and administrative costs alone would be staggering. But, instead of selling and supporting individual outlets, he might opt to sell off sub-franchising rights to several large regions.

Assume the franchisor finds a sub-franchisor willing to pay $100,000 for the right to sub-franchise in one of the regions. In one fell swoop, the franchisor may realize as much income as he would have by selling ten individual outlets, yet without any of the recruiting, training, or administrative overhead. When franchisees begin paying royalties, however, the franchisor and sub-franchisor must divide the payments. Thus, although he maximizes his short-term income, the area franchisor also sacrifices a share of his long-term cash flow.

Trade-name Franchises

Another hybrid form of franchising is the *trade-name franchise*. In a trade-name franchise, the franchisor licenses a franchisee to use a particular name or trademark, plus any number of peripheral items, such as menus, recipes, or advertising aids.

Coca-Cola is easily the most recognizable trade-name franchise. Bottlers buy the right to use the Coke name and obtain access to the "secret" syrup. But they do not receive a comprehensive business-format package. In fact, a typical soft drink bottler may execute contracts with more than one franchisor. Hence, in some localities, the same company that has the Coca-Cola franchise may also bottle Dr. Pepper and Orange Crush.

Obviously, a trade-name franchise must have a well-recognized name or trademark to justify its value.

As you launch your quest for the perfect franchise opportunity, be sure to determine exactly what type of franchise is being offered, and what type is best for you. Do you need or desire training? Is a pre-packaged business format important to you? Or is a famous name or trademark enough? Do you want direct access to the franchisor, or are would you be content dealing with a sub-franchisor or area franchisee? The following list is designed to help you ask — and answer — these and other important questions about the price of admission.

Fees and Royalties: Things to Consider

Initial Fee

- What is the amount of the initial franchise fee?
- Does part of the fee represent goodwill? If so, how much?
- How was the price of goodwill determined?
- Is the price of goodwill reasonable? (to find out, take a look at the potential annual profits of the business, then multiply the projected annual profits times 2.5 to estimate the market value. Now, if the franchise is well established or widely known, is the price of goodwill reasonable — no higher than 12% of the market value of the business? If the franchise is small or new, is the price of goodwill no higher than 4% of the market value of the business?)
- Does part of the initial fee represent the value of a marketing area or sales territory? If so, what is the amount?
- How does the territory price compare with those of other franchises in different territories?
- How much of the initial fee represents the franchisor's costs of:
  Recruiting and advertising?
  Training?
  Site selection assistance?
  Grand Opening assistance?
  The franchise operating manual?
  Signs and other aids?
  Accounting and administration?
- Is the initial fee higher or lower than other comparable franchises in the same industry and with the same number of outlets?

Franchise Royalty

- How does the franchise royalty compare with royalties offered by other franchises in the same industry and with the same number of outlets?
- Is the royalty based on:
  Gross revenues (before expenses)?
  Net sales (after expenses)?

61

Co-op Advertising Royalty

- Does the franchisor charge a co-op ad royalty in addition to the franchise royalty? If not, is part of the franchise royalty used for advertising?
- Does the franchisor design and oversee co-op advertising on behalf of its franchisees?
- What portion of your franchise advertising, if any, will you be responsible for on your own?
- How much does the franchisor spend to advertise and promote its franchises in a year?
- What media are used? How will the selected advertising media reach customers in your market?

Franchise Organization

- Is the franchise a direct satellite of the franchisor, or a unit of a sub-franchisor or area franchisee?
- Does the organization provide you with direct access to the franchisor's staff?
- How often will a franchise representative visit your outlet to offer on-site advice and assistance?
- Is the franchise royalty in line with the level of benefit and assistance afforded by the organization?

Section Two

The Franchise Quest

"In the veins of mountains, beneath building bases
Coined and uncoined, there's gold in many places.
Who, you ask, will bright it to the light?
Man, endowed with Mind's and Nature's might."

Goethe

Chapter Five

Dangling Karats

How Franchisors Recruit Franchisees

George H. first noticed an ad for a Jolly Journeys travel agency franchise in the Wednesday edition of the *Wall Street Journal*. George had always wanted to be a travel agent, and he definitely liked the idea of becoming his own boss. A Jolly Journeys franchise looked like just the right opportunity to combine both ambitions. At the bottom of the ad, in small print, was a phone number to call for more information. It was a long-distance toll call.

Why, George wondered with pique, would any self-respecting franchise company, in an era of global communications and telemarketing, not use a toll-free telephone number? Yet despite the nuisance, George called to inquire about a franchise and to request a copy of the Uniform Franchise Offering Circular, which, as discussed earlier, informs prospective franchisees about the franchisor's background and the mutual obligations created by the franchise agreement.

Instead, what George received in the mail a week later was a packet of brochures, photographs, and application forms. The brochure contained an upbeat description of the benefits of becoming the "president" of a Jolly Journeys travel company. George liked the sound of that: the president of a company, not just a small-time "owner/operator."

Accompanying the brochure was a photograph showing someone about George's age standing happily behind a computer terminal. Yes, George nodded, that could easily be him standing behind that terminal. It looked like a pretty good place to be spending time.

When he unfolded the set of application forms, George's heart sank. There were forms about his personal background, forms about his bank and credit accounts, one for listing his assets, another for his debts and liabilities, still more with essay-type questions about his life ambitions and personal qualifications.

Already, the seemingly simple job of looking at a franchise opportunity was considerably more complicated — and more demanding — than he had ever imagined.

It took George three weeks to get around to completing all the forms and questionnaires. When he mailed them back, he hoped for a prompt response. But when two weeks went by without an acknowledgment, he impatiently called the long-distance phone number. The telephone representative assured George that someone would be getting back to him before long. Three days later, another franchise representative called to thank George for his application and to ask a few personal questions about his job, his family, and his finances.

Six weeks later, George received a Jolly Journeys offering circular and franchise agreement by registered mail. The cover letter invited him for a personal interview at the franchise headquarters in Chicago.

George was dismayed. What he had been expecting was a representative of the franchise company calling on George in his hometown. Now, George was faced with the prospect of spending a sizable sum on round-trip air fare for himself, his wife, and possibly his attorney, as well as food and lodging for the entire party.

By the time George experienced his first eye-to-eye confrontation with his prospective franchisor, he would already have committed numerous hours of self-evaluation and a substantial amount of hard-earned dollars. Those commitments alone would make it hard for him *not* to buy the franchise.

If you've seen or read other books about franchising, you know that most of them talk about how franchise buyers go about finding worthwhile opportunities. But none of them offer any insight into how franchisors go about attracting franchisees and convincing them to sign an agreement. As a result, someone actively engaged in a franchise search is at a decided disadvantage at the bargaining table — unless, of course, he has read this chapter of *The Complete Franchise Book.*

Franchisors use a variety of "secret" strategies to motivate people to apply for a franchise. Many of these strategies follow the psychological principles of "reverse selling," a powerful technique for selling highly priced commodities. In this chapter, we will examine what reverse selling means, why it works, and how franchisors use it to their advantage. Knowing these principles will help you prepare a buying strategy of your own, assuring you equal ground in the tough negotiations ahead.

The Ideal Franchisee

Franchisors intentionally groom their franchise offerings to stimulate the applicant's desire to be his own boss and derive self-esteem from the business. But the bottom line is convincing a potential franchisee that his chances of succeeding depend on buying the franchise.

Hence, a franchisor considers the perfect franchisee to be someone who does *not* possess the complete repertoire of administrative and entrepreneurial skills that it takes to start, develop, and operate a viable business. The "ideal" franchise buyer is more likely to be a front-line supervisor or middle manager than a self-starter or over-achiever.

When a franchisor sets out to recruit franchisees, he adds other, more arbitrary traits to his "ideal franchisee" profile. Franchisors know specifically what age, education, and personal and professional background an individual must possess to be successful in their line of business. Franchisees tend to come from an industry related to the franchise, but many have little previous experience in the business. So the franchisor also tries to identify what type of current job or business a good prospect might have.

The franchisor's recruitment program targets those who are most likely to fit the ideal franchisee profile. The program must grab their attention, motivate them to apply, stimulate them to invest, and sustain their motivation after they sign. The process of applying and interviewing for a franchise can be difficult and time-consuming, and it's no minor challenge to successfully sustain an applicant's motivation from start to startup.

To do so, a franchisor caters not just to the franchisee's rational considerations but also to the emotional. He knows that a prospect must

67

literally fall in love with the business, investing not just working capital but also loyalty, devotion, and self-esteem.

When you open a franchise, in all likelihood you will devote the majority of your waking hours to the business. You will spend more time in the franchise outlet than in your home. The franchise will become an extension of your personality and, as such, your primary source of pride and self-image. Aware of this aspect of your decision, franchisors work hard to attend to the emotional aspects of your franchise search.

Not everyone who has the financial resources to buy a franchise has the desired supervisory, entrepreneurial, and managerial qualities. So, a franchisor must be able to pinpoint the precise segment of the population that has the right behavioral qualifications, is compatible with the franchisor's own management style and personality, and qualifies financially. To accomplish these objectives, the franchisor focuses his advertising and recruiting on those who fit the profile.

The Franchisee Profile

Who are the "ideal" franchisees? As we saw in Chapter Two, the typical franchise owner has at least five years of previous managerial experience, or three or more years in a teaching or training position. He must be a competent learner, but also a good motivator/trainer. As the chief executive of his own business, he has the ultimate responsibility for hiring, training, and motivating employees. Without skills in these areas, a prospective franchisee has little hope of succeeding.

Most franchisees with management backgrounds come from the industry in which the franchisor does business. Individuals tend to start businesses close to their hearts. The ideal apparel-store franchisee is often a would-be fashion designer. A typical video-store owner is a make-believe Hollywood film director. And the perfect owner of an automobile service franchise is a former Indy 500 race driver.

Franchisors decide early in the recruitment process what type of education and marital background their franchisees should possess. Consider, as an example, a franchise to sell toiletries door-to-door. The franchisor may give added weight to married females with no children. The reasoning is that a wife seeking a second source of household income is the most likely to be successful at this kind of business. Furthermore, a married woman without children tends to be more career-oriented than a working mother.

As another example, consider a franchise to operate a retail hardware store. The franchisor might give preference to married male applicants with children on the supposition that the entire family will help run the business. Married fathers also tend be more stable than single males.

It should be clear by now that, when it comes to equal opportunity, granting a franchise is quite different from hiring an employee. A franchisor may set arbitrary standards on the types of persons with whom he enters into a franchise agreement. A franchisee is an independent contractor, not an employee or agent of the franchisor. Certainly, no franchisor should base a recruitment decision on ethnic or sexual prejudice. But franchisors are generally free to select the parties with whom they sign contracts without regard to the criteria that govern employment situations.

Besides demographics, franchisors weigh other, less obvious aspects of your behavior. In some businesses, verbal communication skills, mechanical aptitude, and math skills are important to success. Most franchisors look for evidence of basic organizational skills and strong personal integrity.

Your previous background will weigh heavily in the franchisor's decision to grant you a franchise. Besides management or teaching experience, a franchisor may also be on the lookout for an applicant already familiar with the industry in which the franchise operates.

For instance, a well-known computer-store franchisor considers only applicants who have at least three years of experience in the electronics industry. Other franchisors, however, may study a prospect's background with the opposite view in mind: to eliminate applicants with pre-existing experience in the franchisor's field. For example, some franchisors in the fast-food industry automatically disqualify applicants with a restaurant background.

These franchisors adopt the posture that a freshly trained recruit from outside the industry is more likely to make a successful franchisee. For one thing, he is less apt to bring to the business habits and prejudices inconsistent with or even prohibited by the franchisor's format. For another, his primary source of industry expertise will be his franchisor, further reinforcing the important psychological bond between the parties.

The Three Commitments

It's worth repeating that, as a prospective franchisee, you must really make three types of commitment. The first, of course, is the financial commitment to pay the initial fee, undertake the cost of building and sustaining the business, and giving up a share of the gross revenues. But before you make this fundamental commitment, you must also make two others: one *intellectual*, the other *emotional*.

You must come to grips intellectually with the realities of starting, developing, and managing a business. You must rationally accept the long hours, the extra effort, the operational headaches, and the burdensome paper work. You must understand and be willing to accept the performance standards, restrictions, requirements, and operating procedures of your franchisor. You must be prepared to sacrifice some measure of freedom in exchange for the franchisor's ready-to-go business format. When you actually apply for a franchise with the intention of purchasing it, you must demonstrate your understanding and acceptance early in the recruitment process.

The second type of commitment, the emotional, is far more subtle. Owners often have a true love/hate relationship with their businesses. Invariably, the relationship starts with love. They love the industry, the product, and the image and identity the business bestows upon them. Hate may enter the picture when the franchisee realizes the relationship may not progress exactly as planned, and may even turn sour.

As a prospective franchisee, you too must assess your emotional investment in the business. Project yourself into the franchise environment. How do you feel about spending the majority of your waking hours there? How do you feel about the sign, the building, the store, or the office? Do they inspire pride, enthusiasm, self-esteem? Will you be proud to call yourself the owner of the business, or the president of the company? How do you feel about the franchisor and his staff? Do they inspire loyalty, motivation, confidence? Will you be able to work with — not against — your franchisor for the entire term of the agreement?

If you answer "no" to any of these questions, the franchise is probably not right for you. Likewise, a franchisor can ill afford to grant a franchise to someone who is less than inspired about the industry, the company, and the business.

Motivating Successful Franchising Behavior

When a franchisor is recruiting, he is constantly searching for evidence of successful franchising behavior. Franchisors look to psychological marketing strategies to help cull the field of applicants and potential applicants in the hope of producing a small set of highly qualified, strongly motivated prospects — the *crème de la crème*. The instrument of this strategy is the technique we referred to earlier as "reverse selling."

Reverse selling motivates the prospect to do the selling, effectively reversing the classical roles of customer and salesman. The customer assumes the active role — the salesman takes the resistive role. It's not that the franchisor doesn't want to sell the franchise. He simply wants the prospect to demonstrate enthusiasm, commitment, and perseverance, all essential franchising behaviors. A good franchisee has to be a good salesman, and his first job is to sell himself to the franchisor.

A best-odds franchisee can't resist a challenge. Moreover, he pursues it to its favorable conclusion, overcoming any and all obstacles between himself and his conscious goal. In a reverse-selling scenario, the prospective franchisee has ample opportunity to demonstrate these critical traits. An applicant unwilling or unable to answer the simple challenges posed by the application process has little chance of contending successfully with the everyday realities of owning a small business.

For these reasons, the typical franchisor's recruiting program is designed as a series of psychological obstacles. The prospect must successfully overcome each one in order to advance to the next level of processing. Only after conquering all and demonstrating both an intellectual and emotional commitment does he make the franchisor's list of best-odds franchisees. If he fails to respond appropriately at any point in the process, his name is automatically scratched from the list.

In the illustration which opened this chapter, George, the travel company franchisee, faced a number of carefully devised psychological obstacles. He always had to phone long-distance to communicate with his prospective franchisor. He was required to fill out a barrage of application forms, including time-consuming essay-type questionnaires, before he received any concrete information about the franchise. Finally, he had to decide whether or not to invest in a trip to franchise headquarters.

Overcoming these obstacles placed George on the path to reverse selling. With each subsequent action and commitment, he unconsciously transformed himself from the customer into the salesman. By performing concrete tasks, *he actively pursued the sale*, generating a snowballing surge of psychological momentum that would be difficult to stop.

In this way, a reverse-selling strategy helps to control the franchisor's recruiting costs. Instead of spending thousands to ferret out every potential franchisee, the franchisor can focus on highly specific media that target his most likely prospects. From there, the applicants themselves expend most of the time and money required to consummate the close. Reverse selling develops motivation: By the time the prospect finally overcomes the last obstacle, he is primed with energy and commitment. This emotional "super-charging" bolsters his odds of success.

What kinds of obstacles can you expect to face as a prospective franchisee? How can you reverse the scenario to place yourself at maximum advantage in the negotiating chair? And what warning signals might the franchisor inadvertently give off as he places the obstacles in your path? In the next chapter, we'll examine in detail the process of applying for a franchise, preparing you for an emotional roller coaster ride on the path to a franchise agreement.

Meanwhile, the following list contains some important self-evaluation questions to help you gauge your financial, intellectual, and emotional commitments.

The Three Commitments: Questions to Ask Yourself

Financial

- Overall, does the business seem worth the initial investment?
- Do you think the initial fee fairly reflects the franchisor's costs of putting you in business?
- Are you willing to pay the franchise royalty every month from your gross revenues?
- After deducting your royalty payments, will you still be able to earn a decent profit?
- Can you handle the investment?

Rational

- What does the franchisor offer that you can't otherwise do or achieve by yourself?
- Will the value of the business increase over the years?
- Does the franchisor have a solid track record?
- Are the franchisor's other franchisees satisfied with their investments?

Emotional

- If you buy the franchise, will you be proud to be its owner?
- If you had your choice of any business to enter, would you pick the one in which the franchise is engaged?
- Do you have a special interest or hobby related to the business or trade?
- Are you excited about belonging to this field?

Chapter Six

Search and Research

The Franchise Roller Coaster

Applying for a franchise is like riding a roller coaster. One moment, you're skyrocketing with anticipation, the next you're plummeting into remorse. Now you're ambitious and effusive, now you're cautious and reserved. In one instant you're ready to sign anything, in another you're glancing around furtively, looking for an exit.

The franchise roller coaster ride doesn't happen by accident. It's a contrivance based on carefully researched psychological principles and designed to elicit and control your big-ticket buying behavior.

The Psychological Challenge

In Chapter Five, we saw how the technique known as "reverse selling" motivates prospective franchisees to assume the active role in the sale of the franchise. In this technique, the process of advertising for and recruiting new franchisees takes the form of a series of psychological obstacles the prospect must overcome to consummate the close.

The obstacles range from minor nuisances to significant commitments. For instance, as a prospect, you must always inquire about franchise opportunities at your own expense — never, as George discovered in Chapter Five, by means of a toll-free phone number or postage-paid reply card. Someone who is unwilling to commit to even the minor expense of a long-distance phone call is unlikely either to buy a franchise or to be successful at running one. On the opposite side of the reverse-selling coin, the franchisor who uses persuasive selling tactics may have something to hide. Most likely, he sells franchises to anyone willing to buy. *Beware of the franchisor who makes it too easy to buy a franchise.*

Franchising is a mutual success formula. As a franchise owner, you may succeed or fail depending in large part on the franchisor's competitive strength; that strength, in turn, is derived from the performance of individual franchisees. Hence, a franchisor has to be picky about who purchases a franchise.

The Franchise Recruitment Ad

The classical instrument for attracting best-odds franchise prospects is the franchise recruitment ad. Figure 6-1 shows a hypothetical example. This illustration is a composite of various advertising tactics used by different franchisors to motivate prospective franchisees. (In states regulating franchises, a franchise ad must pass bureaucratic inspection. Guarantees of success or vague claims of financial windfalls are specifically prohibited.)

Ads like the one in the illustration appear every day in business and financial tabloids. The *Wall Street Journal* and *U.S.A. Today* have classified advertising sections devoted specifically to franchise opportunities. Periodicals such as *Inc.* and *Venture*, which target well-capitalized, entrepreneurially motivated individuals, also run franchise ads. In addition, a franchisor may use a trade publication or hobby magazine to reach people experienced in a particular industry.

The example illustrates several psychological aspects of a franchisor's marketing strategy. Franchise ads often avoid referring to the business as a "franchise." Because of past abuses, the term franchising sometimes strikes a negative chord in a potential investor. Moreover, there are thousands of so-called "franchises" on the market. To set the franchisor's opportunity apart, the ad may refer to the franchisee as the "president" of his own business or the "owner" of an outlet. These terms denote a higher level of esteem. Everyone wants to be a "company president," but not everybody would like to be known as a "franchisee." Similarly, the franchise is often referred to as a "company," "store," or "local headquarters." Such euphemisms are employed to capitalize on your drive to be your own boss — and to be perceived by your peers as a VIP.

Every good franchise ad ends with a call to action, a command to perform some activity: "call," "write," "send," "grow," "lead," "inquire," "buy," etc. You'll note that the sample ad ends with an element of mystery. The whole story remains untold, motivating even the most casual reader to wonder.

Figure 6-1
Composite example of a franchise ad

We'll Get You Growing

Widget World Franchise Corporation introduces the first Widget Store, a business for the modern age. But a Widget Store is more than a retail business . . . it's your opportunity to experience self-management, growth, and personal enrichment.

A Widget World Store Owner is a business and community leader. We are currently seeking qualified applicants to own and operate Widget World Stores in selected geographical markets.

Widget World Store Owners benefit from comprehensive training, site-selection assistance, co-op advertising, and on-going guidance. If you think you may qualify, we invite you to explore the Widget World franchise opportunity. Find out how you can participate in the widget revolution that is changing the way people work, relax, and learn.

Director of Franchising
Widget World Franchise Corporation
(415) 555-1012

Yet every ad concludes with a minor obstacle. Either you have to write for more information, or call a long-distance number at your expense. Again, it often pays to beware of the franchisor with a toll-free 800 number: If it's easy to apply, just how selective can the franchisor be? If a franchise company is not selective, how successful can its organization be?

The Franchise Application

Applicants must also contend with a glut of paper work, often seemingly irrelevant. As we have seen, such documentation is meant to ferret out tire-kickers and motivate those with serious intent. It also provides a concrete tool for testing a prospect's organizational and communication skills.

Assume, for instance, that you received a packet of forms from a franchisor and are sitting down to fill them out. Let's say you hastily scribble a few incomplete sentences in pencil. You can be assured the franchisor will believe you are impatient and lack self-esteem. Now let's say you neatly type all your responses in carefully planned, grammatically correct paragraphs. The franchisor is sure to be impressed by your ability to organize your thoughts, plan your activities, and communicate your objectives.

How an individual finishes an essay-type questionnaire reveals as much about his character and personality as a personal interview.

For example, put yourself behind the desk of a franchise sales director reviewing a mountain of applications forms to identify a likely prospect. Compare the answers in the questionnaire in Figure 6-2 to the ones in Figure 6-3.

The applicant who completed the first questionnaire doesn't care how much work it takes to decipher his writing. Moreover, he probably doesn't communicate instructions well, making him a poor trainer and supervisor. Overall, his answers seem poorly prepared, with no definite objective, indicating a poor organizer and a hesitant decision maker. He doesn't seem to care what kind of image his work conveys to others. What kind of image will he project for the franchise system?

In contrast, the questionnaire in Figure 6-3 looks well planned and carefully executed. Not only does the author care about his image but he organizes his thoughts before attempting to communicate them to others. The fact that he committed the extra time and energy to formulate meticulous responses means he is serious about the franchise. He is also serious about how others perceive him. He seeks rapport, acknowledgment, respect.

If you were a franchisor, which of the two applicants would you rather have as a franchisee?

Figure 6-2

Franchise Questionnaire

Briefly describe in your own words the skills which, in your opinion, characterize an effective salesperson:

Getting folks to buy.

How do you propose to finance the business?

Savings account and borrowing.

Have you ever owned a business before, or do you now operate a retail establishment? If yes, please explain:

Used to be an independent rep.

Have you ever been a franchisee of another franchise organization? If yes, please explain in detail:

No.

79

Figure 6-3

Franchise Questionnaire

Briefly describe in your own words the skills which, in your opinion, characterize an effective salesperson:

> Strong communication skills; the gift of verbal persuasiveness. A competent sales pro researches his customer and understands the customer's needs. He creates a need, answers objections, and asks for the business. The personal rapport between salesman and customer is the bottom line.

How do you propose to finance the business?

> | | |
> |---|---|
> | Cash value of life insurance | $45,000 |
> | Savings account | 30,000 |
> | Financial assistance/mortgage | 10,000 |

Have you ever owned a business before, or do you now operate a retail establishment? If yes, please explain:

> Yes. From January, 1979 until July, 1984, I owned a retail computer store with two partners. During this period, we expanded net sales from $2000 per month to $9800 per month.

Have you ever been a franchisee of another franchise organization? If yes, please explain in detail:

> No.

As a final obstacle, a franchisor usually requires a serious applicant to visit the company's headquarters for a personal interview. You can expect the visitation to be conducted at your own expense. If a franchisee's residence is conveniently close to franchise headquarters, the franchisor may even move the interview site to a remote, less convenient location. This last, crucial qualifier separates the committed prospect from the casual tire-kicker.

Lead Processing

From the franchisor's point of view, every person who inquires about a franchise opportunity is a "lead." The series of steps that attract, motivate, and close prospective franchises is therefore a classic case of "lead processing." Figure 6-4 illustrates the four phases of franchise lead processing.

In the first phase, laying the foundation, the franchisor plants his seeds in the marketplace. He establishes awareness of the franchise name, business, and product with an extensive advertising campaign. He next conditions the public to perceive his business as a dominant influence in his industry, usually with a series of newspaper and magazine articles strategically placed by his public relations agent. The third phase is educating the target audience about the advantages and benefits of the franchise program. More ads and more articles help to deliver the message. The four-step chain of events culminates in a "call to action," in which the franchisor literally asks for applicants.

When inquiries begin filtering in by mail, by phone, and in the form of drop-in visits, the franchisor sends out a packet of brochures and forms. Every franchisor has its own "franchise kit." It usually contains a word-processed cover letter, a color brochure, photographs, reprints, and a set of application forms. Most franchisors wait until the application forms are returned before selecting the few prospects who will receive UFOC packages.

Reverse Lead Processing

Often, a prospect requests kits from scores of different franchisors. Just as a franchisor compares the credentials of numerous prospective franchisees, an applicant can compare the offerings of numerous franchising companies and evaluate them against a checklist of franchise-success criteria. Turn-about, after all, is fair play.

The franchise kit will tell you a lot about the franchisor. Its depth, detail, preparation, and professionalism are telltale signs of the franchisor's own self-image, personality, and managerial skills.

Figure 6-4

Four Phases of Franchisee Recruitment

Awareness

The franchisor advertises heavily with as much frequency and reach as his budget permits. The objective is to make you aware of his business.

Dominance

The franchisor positions himself against his competition. The objective is to make you believe his business is superior to others.

Education

The franchisor conducts massive public relations campaigns in the media. The objective is to inform you about the franchise offering.

Response

The franchisor runs franchise ads and disseminates franchise kits. The objective is to get you to apply.

The classical franchise kit consists of five parts:

- A history of the franchising company or its predecessor.
- An overview of the franchise offering, stressing the benefits to franchisees.
- Qualifications for becoming a franchisee.
- Credibility devices, such as ad reprints, photographs, and product samples.
- A set of application forms.

The history is usually told in a brief and colorful description of the founding, growth, and development of the parent firm. What is said is often less relevant than what is *not* said. Watch out for the franchisor who is "short on history," but "long on future." When a franchising venture is so new it has no history, the founder's ad men reach deep into their repertoire of superlatives and positive imagery to create the impression of a lengthy and profitable enterprise. For example, you may find the history of the industry or the history of franchising substituting for a corporate history.

The franchise history almost always focuses on an individual, usually the founder of the company or a famous public figure associated with the franchise. The idea is that franchisees can relate more easily to a human being than to a corporation. Franchisors know a prospect will project his own identity into the franchise, and the historical individual serves as a role model. The premise of a "father figure" at the helm of the franchising company is an important element of the franchisor's recruiting scheme.

The franchise father figure invariably exudes confidence, wisdom, assurance, and security. Before you fall for this strategy, check on the figurehead's background and credentials. Is he or she the real architect of the franchise idea, or simply some actor or model or singer under contract to promote the business?

The overview should include a breakdown of the franchisee's initial investment. Invariably, it enumerates the ostensible benefits of a franchise without mentioning the obligations and restrictions created by the franchise agreement. These "negatives" are left to the UFOC, which only the most highly qualified applicants receive ten business days before the close. (The exact legal requirements for disclosing the information contained in the UFOC are discussed in Chapter Seven.)

To put prospects on the road to reverse-selling behavior, the kit usually includes a lengthy discussion of the qualifications for becoming a franchisee. In this discussion,the franchisor lists the attributes he considers essential to successful franchising behavior.

The usual terms are "leadership," "the quest for independence," and "a desire for self-fulfillment." You won't find any financial promises or guarantees of success. Franchise regulations specifically prohibit blue-sky claims of overnight success or unlimited riches. If you find phrases like "guaranteed success" or "big money opportunity" in a franchise kit, consider them at best unreliable, at worst illegal.

To help you project your identity into the franchise business, the franchise kit may include color photographs, reprints of newspaper or magazine articles about the franchise, or pictures of the outlet or sign. The idea is to help you imagine yourself in the environment of the franchise business. As you scrutinize the photographs or articles, ask yourself this: Is this the kind of place you want to spend most of your waking hours for the foreseeable future?

If a kit doesn't include any of these supplemental materials, you might ask yourself: why not? Can't the franchisor afford color photographs? Or is the company's image so shabby it doesn't want you to see what an actual outlet looks like? Hasn't the franchise been successful enough to get written up in even a small, local newspaper or trade publication? Or doesn't the franchisor have the resources to pay for reprints? A franchise kit may include ad reprints to prove that the franchisor has a strong marketing program. If the kit doesn't have an example, is it because the franchisor is ashamed of its own advertising?

The application forms provide the mechanism for evaluating your successful franchisee behavior. They should include at least three items: (1) a franchise application, similar to an employment application form, requesting basic background information and vital statistics; (2) a personal financial statement, documenting the applicant's assets, liabilities, bank account information, and net worth; (3) an essay-type questionnaire, similar to the ones in Figures 6-2 and 6-3.

Occasionally, a UFOC will be sent to a prospective franchisee in lieu of a franchise kit. However, most franchisors consider their UFOCs to be company secrets and are only willing to deliver them to the most highly qualified prospects. The franchise kit is the franchisor's tool for identifying those prospects. Remember, the franchisor who makes it too easy to apply may be the one who sells indiscriminately, without regard to the buyer's chances of succeeding.

The Selection Process

Only a small percentage of those receiving franchise kits complete and return the application forms. Statistics show that only one person in 2,000 who see a franchise ad are likely to inquire; of these, one in twenty will actually fill out an application. Roughly a third of those who apply for a franchise meet the franchisor's financial, demographic, and behavioral qualifications.

When the franchisor receives an application, he relates the applicant's credentials to the company's predefined success criteria. Figure 6-5 shows an example of a form used by a franchisor to evaluate applicants. In the example, each criterion is assigned a certain weight. As the recruitment specialist evaluates the applicant's materials, he rates the prospect on a scale of one to ten, ten denoting the highest likelihood of success, one indicating the lowest. He then multiplies the evaluation times the weight factor to produce an "index."

When the prospect has been evaluated with respect to all the criteria, the indices are summed to arrive at a final score. The scores of different applicants are then compared, and the top three in a given territory are submitted to the marketing director or chief executive for consideration. These three applications represent the prospective franchisees who will be invited to headquarters for a personal interview.

By this time, the prospect has overcome all the psychological obstacles; he has demonstrated the aggressiveness, enthusiasm, and perseverance that characterize successful franchisees. He has also exhibited ambition, organization, and self-esteem. Yet the largest single obstacle — and the one requiring the greatest personal commitment — still lies ahead: the personal visit.

A Ride on a Roller Coaster

When a prospect arrives at franchise headquarters for a personal interview, his emotional state is highly volatile. Imagine yourself stepping from a plane to the greeting of a seasoned franchise representative. In the first place, you're a little frazzled and probably nervous. In the second, you're full of expectation. What you may fail to realize, however, is that in any major investment decision, buyers undergo a series of emotional peaks and valleys. At one point, you'll be highly energetic, almost wildly optimistic. At another, you'll be cautious, weary, nearly remorseful.

The franchisor tries to control this fluctuation by providing pre-defined stimuli at key points in the interview. For example, at one point, you may view a videotape or slide presentation while seated in a comfortable, overstuffed leather chair. The music and color stimulate your subconscious reactions and the roller coaster begins to climb. Some time later, you sit down for an exhausting interview with a panel of department managers.

The session sets off an emotional plunge. Next comes a tour of a "typical" franchise outlet, sparkling clean and of course crowded with apparent customers. This new "high" only precedes another "low" brought on by a dry and frankly boring contract negotiation with a franchise legal expert.

Figure 6-5

Prospective Franchisee Evaluation Criteria

Criterion	Weight	Evaluation					Index
		Exc.	Good	Avg.	Fair	Poor	
Experience	(.25)						
Sales experience	.10	10	7	5	3	1	_____
Previous bus. owner	.05	10	7	5	3	1	_____
Managerial experience	.05	10	7	5	3	1	_____
Job history and stability	.05	10	7	5	3	1	_____
Aptitude/Attitude	(.25)						
Understanding of sales	.05	10	7	5	3	1	_____
Communication	.05	10	7	5	3	1	_____
Organization	.05	10	7	5	3	1	_____
Ambition/ motivation	.05	10	7	5	3	1	_____
Self-esteem	.05	10	7	5	3	1	_____

Criterion	Weight	Evaluation					Index
		Exc.	Good	Avg.	Fair	Poor	
Personal	(.25)						
Financial history	.08	10	7	5	3	1	_____
Arrest record	.08	10	7	5	3	1	_____
References	.02	10	7	5	3	1	_____
Marital/family history	.02	10	7	5	3	1	_____
Stability	.05	10	7	5	3	1	_____
Financial	(.25)						
Net worth	.15	10	7	5	3	1	_____
Financial outlook	.10	10	7	5	3	1	_____
					TOTAL RANKING		_____

From the franchisor's point of view, the idea is to control your emotions. When they're on a sharp upturn, the franchise sales director will offer the contract for signing. The closing always takes place on an optimistic peak, never in a pessimistic valley.

As a prospective franchisee, you want to maintain an even keel to prevent the franchisor's marketing experts from controlling your emotions and guiding your buying behavior. Similarly, you must recognize that buyer's remorse is a natural part of any major investment decision.

Sales pressure from a franchise marketing staff can be extremely low key. You may not be pressured to sign; in fact, you may be discouraged. Again, this discouragement is part of the franchisor's reverse-selling strategy. The real aim is to take away the franchise so you'll scramble hurriedly to grab it back.

A favorite tactic of franchise salesmen is the technique known as "false urgency." When this strategy is in effect, you have only a few days to sign, maybe even a few hours: Unless you act at once, you run the risk of losing the franchise to one of scores of other eager applicants.

Due to these inevitable, often subtle, pressure tactics, it's a good idea not to sign any agreement or make any payment at the franchisor's place of business. Wait until you're in your own territory. Give yourself plenty of time to review what you've seen, heard, and read. Share the offering circular and franchise agreement with your attorney and accountant. If you can afford to, take your attorney with you when you visit the franchisor's headquarters. It might also pay to hire a franchise consultant for an insider's opinion on the merits of the franchise.

Be sure you've completed your homework and know exactly what facts, if any, lie hiding behind and between the lines of the franchisor's offering circular. Get the names and addresses of other franchisees, and contact them.

Ask the following questions:

- Is the franchisee satisfied with his franchises?
- How much did he pay for his franchises?
- How much did he pay for furnishings, fixtures, and inventory?
- How do these amounts compare to the prices at which the franchisor offers the same items to you?
- What kind of profits is the franchisee earning?
- What is the amount of his franchise royalty?
- What doesn't he like about the franchise?
- Has the franchisor always "been there" for him?
- Did the franchisor's training program give him a real head start?
- How often does he hear from his franchise representative?
- Is the franchisor reasonable in all his dealings with franchisees?
- Has the franchisor cited the franchisee for any violations, and if so, of what nature?
- If the franchisee had the chance to do it all over again, would he purchase a franchise from the same franchisor today?

To be successful in a franchise, you must love the business as well as understand and finance it. Remember that your emotional commitment is only one of three essential investments you must make in the franchise: emotional, intellectual, and financial. If even one of these ingredients is missing, the franchise is probably not right for you. If they're all there, not only is it probably the right franchise but your chances of succeeding in it are outstanding.

Chapter Seven

Full and Accurate Disclosure

The Rules of Franchising

It was a balmy Florida afternoon in October when Irwin quit his job managing a chain of cafeterias. Withdrawing his life savings, he signed a contract to purchase three franchise locations from SuperFat Franchise Corporation (a fictitious name for a real company). Irwin bought more than franchise rights; he took over three developed restaurants lock, stock, and deep-fat fryer. SuperFat had operated the locations as company-owned outlets for several years. Consequently, Irwin felt he was purchasing a business with a track record, backed by a major franchisor with a national reputation.

What he got was not the elevator to success, but simply the shaft.

Since SuperFat offered the restaurants as part of a franchise package, Irwin paid the company's then-current franchise fee for each location. In addition, he shoveled out close to $300,000 for the buildings, fixtures, and goodwill, and agreed to assume the leases on both properties. To swing the deal, Irwin mortgaged his home, used his savings, and took out a $175,000 loan.

As it turned out, the package price included an exorbitant amount for the restaurants' used furnishings and fixtures — more, in fact, than the price of new equipment from any restaurant supply dealer. To make matters worse, Irwin's contract obligated him to buy all food, napkins, and other supplies from specified vendors; the prices he paid were far greater than the cost of the same items from independent suppliers. (Unknown to Irwin, SuperFat Franchise Corporation received a percentage of the value of every order he placed.)

The reason SuperFat sold off the outlets in the first place? They had never turned a profit.

Four hard years later, Irwin missed a rent payment. Like a drooling vulture perched atop a light tower, SuperFat quickly swooped in to repossess the restaurants. In less than a week, Irwin's investment, livelihood, and great American dream went up in smoke like a scorched double cheeseburger on an unattended grill.

Irwin is a fictitious name, but his story is only too true. Franchising is often called a silver lining in an economic cloud, but it is sometimes more like a dark and threatening thunderhead.

California was the first state to adopt legislation singling out franchisors for regulation. In 1977, the California Franchise Investment Protection Act required franchisors to register with the state Department of Corporations, to comply with a list of disclosures, and to receive authorization from a regulatory agency prior to doing business. Today, fifteen states individually regulate the offer and sale of franchises (more on this later).

In 1980, the Federal Trade Commission instituted comprehensive rules regulating all U.S. franchisors in order to protect investors against unscrupulous practices.

Unfortunately, despite such efforts, it is still possible for an unsuspecting "Irwin" to be taken advantage of today. Although fifteen states regulate franchising, the remaining thirty-five rely on federal regulations alone. The FTC has neither the time nor the manpower to effectively police every possible franchise violation. Even in states where rigid rules and requirements are in force, a problem is not likely to be brought to the attention of the authorities until *after it has occurred*. With the current case loads in the courts, you can expect to wait several years for a franchise dispute to be resolved.

The fact remains that no amount of state or federal regulation can adequately replace the exercise of sound judgment and reasonable caution in the research and negotiation of a franchise agreement. The more you know about the rules, the better prepared you are to recognize the signposts of a come-on or rip-off.

Federal Franchise Rules

The FTC's franchise regulations stem from the Federal Trade Commission Act. Section Five of that law begins, "Unfair methods of competition in commerce, and unfair or deceptive acts or practices in commerce, are declared unlawful."

The same section goes on to empower the commission to bring proceedings against anyone who transgresses an FTC rule or regulation. The landmark FTC rule governing franchise practices is Rule 436.1. The rule declares:

> . . . it is an unfair or deceptive act or practice within the meaning of Section 5 of (the FTC Act) for any franchisor or franchise broker: (a) to fail to furnish any prospective franchisee with the following information accurately, clearly, and concisely stated in a legible written document at the earlier of the "time for making of disclosures" or the first "personal meeting."

In this rule, the phrase "following information" is further defined as a prospectus, or Uniform Franchise Offering Circular (UFOC). The UFOC was originally designed by the Midwest Securities Commissioners Association as a prototype for franchise disclosures. Its purpose is to equip prospective franchisees with information about the franchisor's background and the obligations created by the franchise agreement before any agreement is signed. For this reason, the FTC rule mandates a minimum period of time in which the UFOC must be in the hands of a prospective franchisee before a contract may be executed.

Let's take a closer look at the two key phrases: "the time for the making of disclosures" and "the first personal meeting."

The Time for the Making of Disclosures

Shorn of official language, the "time for the making of disclosures" is ten business days prior to signing of any agreement or the payment of any fee. In other words, it's illegal for a franchisor to sign a franchisee to a deposit/reservation agreement, a purchasing contract, or a leasehold agreement before ten business days have lapsed from the time the franchisee receives the UFOC.

The rule is quite specific on this matter, defining the waiting period as:

> ten (10) business days prior to the earlier of (1) the execution by a prospective franchisee of any franchise agreement or any other agreement imposing a binding legal obligation on such prospective franchisee, about which the franchisor, franchise broker, or any agent, representative, or employee thereof, knows or should know, in connection with the sale or proposed sale of a franchise, or (2) the payment by a prospective franchisee, about which the franchisor, franchise broker or any agent, representative, or employee thereof, knows or should know, of any consideration in connection with the sale or proposed sale of a franchise.

Note the phrase "any consideration in connection" with the franchise. Remember it well when you enter the franchisor's conference room to sit down at the negotiating table.

Unless a franchisee has had at least ten business days to study the UFOC and the franchise agreement, no franchisor may ask, coerce, or encourage him to make any kind of payment. That includes any deposit, down payment, or purchase of inventory relating to the franchise.

Every professional salesperson knows well the meaning of the term "false urgency." A franchise salesman creates false urgency when he tells a prospect he has several potential franchisees waiting in line for the same territory. But if he asks for a deposit to "hold" the franchise before the waiting period (ten business days, i.e., two weeks) has elapsed, the salesman is violating the FTC rule.

The First Personal Meeting

The FTC franchise rule also demands that the franchisor give every prospective franchisee a copy of the UFOC. In the event of a "personal meeting," the document must be handed over at that time. A personal meeting is defined as:

> a face to face meeting between a franchisor or franchise broker (or any agent, representative, or employee thereof) and a prospective franchisee which is held for the purpose of discussing the sale or possible sale of a franchise.

Does that mean franchisors have to give out a UFOC to every "tire-kicker" who walks into a store and inquires about a franchise? Not really. If a franchise salesman comes out grinning, he'd better have a UFOC in his hand. But if there's no one around but a store clerk or receptionist, it's safe just to take the inquirer's name and phone number. The important words are "for the purpose of discussing the sale or possible sale of a franchise." So if you happen to run into a franchise salesman at a barbecue or while tailgating at the ball park, don't expect him to be carrying a tote-bag full of UFOCs.

The Right of Rescission

What if a franchisor should happen to pressure you into signing an agreement before the required waiting period has elapsed? Or what if a franchise salesman fails to give you a UFOC on the day of your first personal meeting? Should you call the police? The FBI?

Though it's a federal crime to violate an FTC rule, it's not very likely a guilty franchisor will be led off in chains. If a franchisor, franchise salesman, or broker fails to abide by the FTC regulations, the franchisee typically has the right to rescind any agreement. In addition, the franchisee will normally be entitled to full compensation for the total amount of his investment, plus any damages he can prove.

State Franchise Regulations

Table 7-1 lists the states that currently regulate franchising. In most of these states, the regulations are considerably more strict than those of the FTC. As with California, most of these states require the franchisor to apply for registration, then await approval from a state authority before beginning to offer franchises. The laws also apply to out-of-state franchisors who do business in the named, regulated states.

In the case where a state law is more stringent than the FTC rules, the state law applies. The California franchise regulations, both the flagship and the prototype for state franchise statutes, contain the following highlights:

● *Franchise Registration*

A franchisor must apply for registration with a government authority before offering franchises in the state. The application must be accompanied by the franchisor's UFOC and an exact copy of the franchise agreement that the franchisor will use in the state. The franchisor's application must be approved by the state before he can offer or sell a franchise.

How does that affect you, the prospective franchisee?

Let's say you live in New York, one of the individually regulated states with a registration requirement. Any New York-based franchise company must register with the state before it may begin offering franchises for sale. But what about an out-of-state franchisor? No matter where his company headquarters, in order to offer you a franchise he must register in New York. Even if this franchisor is based in Nevada — a state which does not require registration — he must still register in New York before offering or selling franchises to New York residents.

But what if the outlet will be located in a different state? If you are a resident of a state which requires registration, the franchisor must still comply with your state's laws even though you may be planning on opening the outlet out of state. If the outlet will be located in a different state which also has a registration requirement, the franchisor must register in that state, as well.

● *Fee Impoundment*

If the state authorities do not find the franchisor's financial statement to be strong enough to fulfill all the promises and obligations created by the franchise agreement, they may impound franchise fees. Under an impoundment order, the franchisor must place the initial fee collected from a franchisee in an escrow account. The funds are released to the franchisor on a state order only after the franchisee signs a statement affirming that the franchisor has fulfilled all his promises and obligations.

So, if you purchase a franchise from a franchisor in a regulated state, and if the franchisor's financial statements do not show a seven-figure net worth, you may find yourself writing out a check to an impoundment account.

Don't panic. It's just your state's method of assuring that you are satisfied with your franchisor's performance before committing your funds to his keeping. A franchise impoundment account is a type of escrow and, as such, may produce interest on any deposited funds. The terms of the impoundment stipulate that the monies will not be released to the franchisor until you, the franchisee, avow in writing that the franchisor has fulfilled all his promises and obligations to your personal satisfaction.

● *Authorization to Advertise*

In many of the regulated states, a franchisor may not place an advertisement to sell or promote a franchise until the state regulatory agency has reviewed and approved the ad. The law requires a franchisor to submit advertising materials, including brochures as well as newspaper or magazine ads, to a regulator, then wait five days for clearance. If no restraining order results, the franchisor may proceed with the ad campaign.

● *Periodic Updates*

Franchisors approved by a regulated state must periodically update their applications in the form of bi-annual amendments. Even if no changes have occurred during the last six months, an update must normally be filed, in order to maintain the franchise registration. Whenever a franchisor sells a franchise, changes a contract provision, or is involved in court activity, he must amend his UFOC and submit an amendment.

Curiously, while most of the states that regulate franchising have similar requirements, the regulatory agencies chosen for the task vary considerably. For example, in New York, the attorney general oversees franchising, but in Washington State, franchisors register with a division of the Department of Motor Vehicles.

Table 7-1

State Agencies Regulating Franchisors

California	Department of Corporations 600 S. Commonwealth Ave. Los Angeles, CA 90005
Connecticut	Securities Division State Office Building Hartford, CT 06115
Illinois	Attorney General 500 S. Second St. Springfield, IL 62706
Indiana	Securities Commissioner 102 State House Indianapolis, IN 46204
Maryland	Division of Securities 26 S. Calvart St., Rm. 602 Baltimore, MD 21202
Michigan	Department of Commerce 6546 Mercantile Way Lansing, MI 48823
Minnesota	Department of Commerce Seventh & Roberts Sts. St. Paul, MN 55101
New York	Department of Law World Trade Center, Rm. 4874 New York, NY 10047
North Dakota	Securities Commission Capital Building, 3rd Floor Bismarck, ND 58505

Rhode Island	Department of Business Regulation 100 N. Maine St. Providence, RI 02903
South Dakota	Division of Securities State Capital Building Pierre, SD 57501
Virginia	Division of Securities 11 S. 12th St. Richmond, VA 23219
Washington	Securities Division P. O. Box 648 Olympia, WA 98504
Wisconsin	Securities Commission P. O. Box 1768 Madison, WI 53701

An Offer Made in This State

An area of particular regulatory confusion is the issue of when a franchise offer is legally made in a regulated state. What if a franchisor advertises in a newspaper that has a circulation in more than one state, and one of the states happens to be a regulated state? What if an offer is made to a franchisee who lives in a regulated state but intends to establish the franchise in another state? What if a franchisor invites a resident of a regulated state to meet in an unregulated state to sign a franchise agreement?

Most state laws follow the lead of the California Franchise Investment Protection Act, which states in Section 31013:

> An offer or sale of a franchise is made in this state when an offer to sell is made in this state, or an offer to buy is accepted in this state, or, if the franchisee is domiciled in this state, the franchised business is or will be operated in this state.

What this paragraph means is that a franchisor falls under state jurisdiction whenever it offers a franchise to a resident, no matter where the offer originates. The law also applies if the franchise will be located in the state, even if the franchisee lives elsewhere.

How about an offer made by a franchisor in a regulated state to a prospective franchisee in an unregulated state? The California law elaborates on this point:

> An offer to sell is made in this state when the offer either originates from this state or is directed by the offeror to this state . . . .

Hence, any offer either going out of the state or coming into it falls under state jurisdiction. But what about a franchise ad in the national edition of the *Wall Street Journal*? If the franchisor has not applied for registration in a regulated state, does the ad violate that state's franchise laws?

Here's how California and most of the other regulated states handle this problem:

> An offer is not made in this state merely because (1) the publisher circulates or there is circulated on his behalf in this state any bona fide newspaper or other publication of general, regular, and paid circulation which has had more than two-thirds of its circulation outside this state during the past 12 months, or (2) a radio or television program originating outside this state is received in this state.

98

This section of the California franchise law exempts a franchise ad in a publication with more than two thirds of its circulation outside the state, or a TV or radio ad with a national audience.

Besides state and federal regulations, the courts also influence the rights of franchisees when they rule on disputes. These decisions affect not only how a franchisor may offer and sell the franchise but the ground rules for purchasing, pricing, and involuntary termination. We'll examine these important issues in Chapter Eleven, when we dissect, translate, and interpret the legal instrument of franchising — the franchise agreement.

Meanwhile, the following list will help you be certain whether or not a prospective franchisor is complying with the rules of franchising.

Franchising by the Rules: Were They Followed?

- Has the franchisor provided you with a Uniform Franchise Offering Circular?
- Was the circular complete and accurate?
- Was the circular accompanied by a copy of the franchisor's most recent audited financial statements?
- Did a copy of the franchise agreement accompany the offering circular?
- Were you pressured into signing the agreement before ten business days had elapsed from the time you received the offering circular?
- Were you pressured into signing any related agreement, such as a deposit or purchase agreement, before the prescribed waiting period had transpired?
- Did the franchisor make any verbal promises that were not consistent with the offering circular?
- Did the franchisor make any promises of profits or earnings?
- If you reside in a regulated state, is the franchisor registered or otherwise cleared to offer or sell franchises in your state?
- If you reside in a state which is not regulated, but the franchise will be located in a regulated state, is the franchisor registered with the state where you plan to open the franchise?

Chapter Eight

Great Revelations

Inside the Uniform Franchise Offering Circular

Secure in his knowledge that Big Brother was looking out for his interests, Paul S. studied his franchisor's Uniform Franchise Offering Circular (UFOC) and duly noted the background and experience of the principals (officers, directors, executives, etc.) They seemed honest enough: apparently none had been sued or indicted, nor had they been involved with any bankrupt or fraudulent businesses. In fact, their records looked "squeaky clean" — just what you'd expect from those you're entrusting with your livelihood and savings.

Unknown to Paul, the president of the franchise corporation had been convicted of shoplifting and child molestation, had once been committed to a mental institution, and was sued for fraud on four different occasions. Moreover, the company's marketing director had gone bankrupt in a previous business.

How was it that none of these astonishing details showed up in the franchise offering circular? Although "full and accurate disclosure" is a requirement of franchisors operating in every state, there are certain limitations on the types of information that must be disclosed. In California, for instance, a criminal record must not be included in a franchise disclosure. In many states, franchisors do not have to divulge unsavory episodes that occurred prior to fifteen years from the date on which the circular was drafted.

Although the UFOC informs prospective franchisees about the proposed investment, it does not completely shield them from potential fraud. The burden of verifying a franchisor's credentials and credibility remains with the franchisee. So don't rely on the UFOC alone; if any gaps appear in the disclosures, ask for a *complete* resume of each of the principals, covering their *entire* business history. The Federal Trade Commission requires all U.S. franchisors to disclose certain information to the public. In cases where the local law or regulation is more severe than the FTC rule, the local restrictions take precedence. As we saw in Chapter Seven, the state rules apply whenever one of the following is true:

a. the franchisor is headquartered in the regulated state,
b. the franchisor plans to offer or sell franchises in the regulated state,
c. a franchise outlet will be opened in the regulated state,
d. a person who purchases a franchise is a resident of the regulated state, even though the outlet may be opened in another state.

But what about franchisors headquartered in one of the states that do not require registration? When they offer or sell franchises to people who live in unregulated states, the important requirements are preparing a UFOC and complying with the FTC's mandated waiting period.

The Disclosure Document

The UFOC is sometimes referred to as the *disclosure document*, because its purpose is to disclose vital information about a franchise opportunity. It presents highlights of the franchise agreement and describes the backgrounds of the franchisor and his associates.

But often, what is said in an offering circular is not as important as what is *not* said. An omission of a pertinent fact is a form of inaccuracy and a violation of the full-and-accurate-disclosure requirement. Nevertheless, omissions do occur, and it is usually difficult to prove in a court of law that they were made with an intent to defraud. Moreover, a UFOC is not policed with the same rigor as, say, a securities prospectus.

102

To see how to evaluate a disclosure document and how to search between the lines for disguised or hidden meanings, let's examine each section of the UFOC separately.

1. The Franchisor and Any Predecessors

The first section is devoted to the franchisor's personal and business names, address, organization, background, and financial history. Any predecessors of the franchising company must also be listed. A "predecessor" means a previous business operated by the franchisor which has a direct relationship to the franchise.

Consider, as an example, a franchisor who once owned a taxicab company before starting a successful toy store. After a few years, he decides to package a franchise program based on his retail toy operation. So, he founds a new company to sell toy store franchises.

In his UFOC, the franchisor must disclose that he owned the original toy store, because that business was a predecessor to the franchising company. But he does not have to disclose his involvement in the taxicab business, since that operation has no relation to the toy store franchise.

Most franchising companies are operated as separate business entities from their original operations. Assume, for example, that an entrepreneur owns a successful health-food restaurant, and he decides to begin selling franchises. He starts a new business whose only activity will be franchising. As a result, he now owns two separate businesses — a health-food restaurant and a franchising company.

The reason a franchisor creates a separate franchising company is to limit his risks. If the franchising business runs into trouble, the original operation may not fail or even be liable for the losses or damages incurred by the franchising operation.

The issue of predecessor companies raises several important questions:

- How long has the franchisor operated a business similar to the proposed franchise outlet?
- What kind of success did the franchisor experience in the business?
- Can that success be duplicated in your locality?
- Were any of the principals involved in an enterprise that might suggest ethical impropriety, poor judgment, or just plain bad management?

If a franchisor has nothing to hide, he will most likely list all the companies he founded or owned prior to developing the franchise.

In addition to his predecessor companies, the franchisor must describe the business of the franchise, the types of customers for this type of product or service, and the competition.

2. Persons Affiliated with the Franchisor

The identity and business experience of the directors, trustees, partners, principals, and other managers of the franchising company must be disclosed in this section. A short biography of each person states name, position, and experience for the last five years.

Note that the rules require a background disclosure for only the five years previous to the effective date of the offering circular. For bankruptcies, the period of disclosure is fifteen years. For example, let's say the vice president of a franchising company was hired three years ago. For the prior three years, he was an executive with a large corporation in the same industry. But before that, he ran a side show for a traveling carnival. Under the franchise rules, only the officer's business background for the past five years has to be disclosed. So, the UFOC would have to list only his positions as vice president of the franchising company and as a corporate executive in the industry. Because his carnival-show period took place more than five years ago, this entire episode may lawfully be omitted from the UFOC. Yet, that fact, if disclosed, might very well influence your final decision whether or not to purchase a franchise from this company.

Naturally, most franchisors disclose only as much information as is legally required. Moreover, the rules actually exempt certain kinds of lawsuits or indictments from having to be disclosed. For example, if your franchisor was sued for not paying his bills, but not for fraud or fraudulent conversion, the incident most likely would not have to be disclosed in the offering circular. Even a suit for fraud, if it occurred more than fifteen years ago, does not have to be disclosed.

Moreover, *California law actually forbids the disclosure of any criminal arrest or conviction.* So, it's possible even for a convicted rapist or a bank robber to appear flawless on a franchise offering circular.

Franchisors who really are squeaky clean are more likely to publish a full declaration of each principal's criminal, financial, and business background in the UFOC, above and beyond the legal time limits for disclosure. If a franchisor's disclosures stick closely to the limits, it's wise not to rely on the UFOC alone to assess such information.

Ask the franchise representative for the complete resumes of all the individuals listed in the offering circular. Bluntly inquire if any of them have *ever* been sued or declared bankrupt. Your franchisor may decline to answer, but it's against the law for him — or any of his representatives or brokers — to lie to you about this, or any other matter related to the franchise. If you don't get the information you ask for, and you feel it's important, you can always break off negotiations and look for a different franchise.

3. Litigation

In this section of the offering circular, the franchisor must describe any criminal or civil actions involving any violation of a franchise law, fraud, embezzlement, or unfair business practices. But any lawsuit which did not specifically involve one of these violations does not have to be disclosed in the UFOC. Since California law forbids the disclosure of a criminal record, in that state only civil actions will appear in a UFOC.

When a criminal or civil action is disclosed, the UFOC must reveal the title and parties of the action, the court, the nature of the claim, and the relationship between the litigating parties. If there is no pending litigation, that, too, should be stated.

In an age of widespread and often casual litigation, the question arises: just how extensive must these disclosures be? Can they be limited to those cases that are pertinent to the franchise business? For example, assume you're the vice president of a franchise corporation and you sell your house to relocate. Several months after escrow closes, the buyer discovers a leak in the roof. Disgruntled, he sues you for fraud, claiming you knew the roof leaked all along. You, of course, claim you had no prior knowledge of the leak. But until the matter is settled, the litigation remains on the books. Does this case have to be disclosed in your company's franchise offering circular?

The rules are clear on this issue. For the franchisor or any director, trustee, partner, officer, financial, marketing, training, or service executive, the offering circular must disclose any *pending* administrative, criminal or material civil action

> . . . alleging a violation of any franchise law, fraud, embezzlement, fraudulent conversion, misappropriation of property or comparable allegations.

Note the rule says "alleging." Even while the case is in dispute, the particulars have to be disclosed. In addition, the UFOC must describe any felony conviction or court injunction relating to the franchise in the last ten years.

4. Bankruptcy

In this section, the franchisor must reveal whether he, any predecessor in the business, or any of his partners or officers have been declared bankrupt in the last fifteen years. Specifically, he must tell whether any of the foregoing have been

> ". . . adjudicated bankrupt or reorganized due to insolvency . . ."

If an individual was an officer or partner in a company that went bankrupt, that, too, must be disclosed. Because personal bankruptcies are so prevalent under present law, it is not uncommon for a franchisor to have at least one principal or executive who has undergone the process of insolvency. For example, the franchise sales director for a well-known franchisor in the transportation field once owned a small shoe store which fell on hard times during the nationwide recession of the late 1970s. But that bankruptcy had no bearing whatsoever on his performance as a sales director for his current employer. So, even though the incident was recorded in the company's UFOC, it was not likely to influence a prospective franchisee's decision.

You should realize that just because a franchisor has in his employ an executive who once declared bankruptcy does not *per se* doom the franchise to failure. But beware of the franchisor who attempts to disguise a past bankruptcy rather than openly disclose it.

5. The Initial Fee or Other Payment

This section of the UFOC states the amount of the franchise fee. The disclosure should also describe the franchisor's provisions for refunds, and state whether the fee is payable in a lump sum or in installments.

For example, some franchise agreements do not allow for the initial fee to be refunded under any conditions. Others provide for fifty percent of the fee to be refunded if the franchisee fails to pass the franchisor's training program. Whereas some franchisors demand the entire initial fee be paid in a single lump sum when the franchise agreement is signed, others will accept or defer partial payments.

The franchisor must also state where the initial fee will end up; usually, it is deposited in the "general funds" of the franchising company. It's common for an offering circular to say that the initial fee is "fully earned by the franchisor." Simply stated, that means when you sign the franchise agreement and pay the initial fee, you agree that you are not entitled to a refund if you decide to back out later.

6. Other Fees

Any other fees or payments, such as the ongoing royalty or advertising fund, must be disclosed in this section of the UFOC. If, after signing a franchise agreement, you end up having to pay special charges or fees not specifically disclosed in the UFOC, there's a possibility your franchisor may have violated the law.

For example, let's say you are considering a franchise for a family-style restaurant. Recognizing that location is important to success in this line of business, the franchisor agrees to select the site for your outlet. Two weeks after you sign the franchise agreement, a representative arrives in your hometown to scout out the trading area. Aided by local real estate consultants, the franchise representative finally picks the "perfect" site for your new restaurant. He even stays around long enough to help you negotiate the lease. Two weeks later, you receive a bill for the representative's air fare, lodging, food, and a "site selection fee."

In cases like this example, the site selection fee and all related charges must be listed in the UFOC for you to inspect before you sign the agreement. Likewise, any similar charges for consultation services, accounting, marketing, or other assistance should be fully and accurately disclosed.

7. Initial Investment

This section of the offering circular breaks down your total initial investment. The breakdown must say exactly who receives each payment item and when it is due. For example, the initial fee is payable to the franchisor, and it is usually due "on signing" the franchise agreement. But a lease deposit for your store or office is paid to your lessor, due "as agreed" by you and the lessor. If the lessor of the site happens to be your franchisor, that fact will appear in this section of the UFOC.

When the initial investment is likely to vary — e.g., due to local economic conditions — a high-low estimate is often made. The high estimate includes the highest initial fee charged by the franchisor, as well maximum amounts for such items as real estate, equipment, and supplies. The low estimate reflects the lowest investment for which a franchisee could conceivably get into the business. However, the low investment breakdown is usually based on costs found only in certain areas of the country, i.e., the most economically depressed markets.

The breakdown may include the cost of real estate, equipment, fixtures, inventory, deposits, or other payments. Figure 8-1 shows an example of a franchisor's estimated initial investment breakdown. The illustration gives an amount for working capital; this figure represents the estimated cash required to sustain the business until it begins to turn a profit. Franchisors are not specifically required to include working capital as part of the initial investment breakdown. If you are considering a franchise and the estimated investment does not include working capital requirements, be sure to ask the franchisor for a low-high estimate.

By omitting working capital, the franchisor produces a seemingly lower cost of getting into the franchise; but it is impossible to start a business without an amount set aside for working capital.

8. Obligations of Franchisee to Purchase or Lease from Designated Sources

In this section of the UFOC, franchisors must disclose whether you will be required to buy any products, equipment, or services either from the franchisor or from a specified source. For example, if you obtain a franchise to open a muffler shop, will you have to purchase and sell only mufflers offered by your franchisor? If you don't have to buy them from your franchisor, will be you forced to buy them from a particular supplier? If so, what is the supplier's connection (if any) with your franchisor?

It is difficult, but not impossible, for a franchisor to force franchisees to purchase equipment, supplies, or inventory from a designated source. In the past, the courts have frowned on such sole-source purchasing obligations, unless it can be proved that the product is so unique it cannot be obtained from any other supplier.

For instance, let's say you're considering a franchise to open a photography studio. The franchisor cannot usually force you to purchase film from either the franchisor or the franchisor's designated supplier. But he can force you to comply with his specifications for film type and quality. You're free to purchase that film from any supplier. But the chances are good that your franchisor — or his designated source — will offer the best combination of availability and pricing. Most franchisors encourage their franchisees to purchase from a designated source by offering discount pricing or other benefits.

9. Obligations of Franchisee to Purchase or Lease in Accordance with Specifications or from Approved Suppliers

This section of the UFOC must disclose whether, as a franchisee, you will be required to buy any products or supplies based on the franchisor's specifications or prior approval. For instance, assume you are considering a franchise to start a computer store, and the franchisor requires that you sell only computers that appear on his "approved product" list. That requirement must be disclosed before you sign the franchise agreement, not after you begin setting up your showroom.

Purchasing standards are usually designed to encourage franchisees to buy particular brands or to use a particular supplier. For example, if you own a video store franchise, your franchisor cannot force you to carry only a certain brand of video cassette recorder. What he *can* do is stipulate a set of specifications that conform to a particular make or model. You have the choice of carrying the product line which conveniently meets the franchisor's specifications, or, as an alternative, investing a few million dollars to manufacture your own version. Now, which option is more attractive?

10. Financing

This section of the UFOC is used to describe any financing arrangements offered by the franchisor or another party associated with the franchise. Many franchisors offer financial assistance to franchisees. Some will finance all or part of your investment, others only the initial fee.

A franchising company that does not offer its own financing arrangement often has ties with a local bank or investment company. For example, let's say you want to buy a franchise, but you'll need a bank loan to swing the deal. The franchisor you have in mind doesn't offer financing, but during your visit to franchise headquarters, you are introduced to an officer of a nearby bank. To your surprise, the banker has already transferred all your financial data from the franchise application onto a loan application. "All you have to do," the loan officer assures you, "is sign."

Sound easy? Maybe *too* easy, you might think. The bank in this example probably handles all the franchisor's banking business. The franchisor may even have agreed to co-sign for the loan. In some cases, the franchisor receives a commission or "finder's fee" for sending the bank new business.

No matter what the arrangement, the details must be disclosed in the UFOC.

11. Obligations of the Franchisor

Under this heading, the franchisor describes the service he promises to provide you after you sign the franchise agreement. The list of services is broken down as follows:

a. services provided prior to opening;
b. other supervision or assistance;
c. services provided while you are open for business;
d. assistance in selecting the site for your outlet.

Also in this section, the franchisor discloses the location and length of the training program, and states exactly who must pay for the travel and living expenses. It may surprise you to learn that most franchisees must pay for their own airline tickets, hotel rooms, and meals while they are attending franchise training school. If that's the case, your obligation must be clearly stated in the UFOC.

A typical franchise training program lasts from one to three weeks. Unless you live in the franchisor's hometown, the cost of travel, lodging, and meals is likely to be considerable. Yet, this cost is almost always excluded from the initial investment breakdown in Section 6 of the UFOC. If you are required to pay for your own transportation and lodging to attend the training program, the UFOC should state a reasonable estimate of the *per diem*, or daily cost.

The following example is extracted from Section 11 of an actual UFOC:

> Franchisee is required to pay his own costs in connection with attending the training program. The cost *per diem*, including lodging and meals, is likely to be ninety dollars ($90) per day.

Like the low estimate in the initial investment breakdown, the cost *per diem* is usually based on budget lodging and inexpensive restaurants. Although you may actually be able to contain your travel costs within this estimate, chances are you won't find the accommodations satisfactory or the meals appetizing. As a general rule, it's a good idea to multiply the franchisor's estimate for lodging and meals by one and a half.

12. Exclusive Territory

In this section of the UFOC, the franchisor must state whether or not you will receive a protected territory as part of your franchise. Will you receive an exclusive territory? Does the franchisor promise not to sell any other franchises in your territory? Can the franchisor sell the same products to customers in your territory by mail order or through any other means?

Territories don't always come with a franchise. When they do, their boundaries may be subject to change. For instance, if you have a franchise to sell cosmetics in a designated part of the city, you might be obligated to maintain a certain sales volume. If you fail to meet the quota, you may find your territory shrinking in size. On the other hand, if you happen to exceed the sales quota, your franchisor might see fit to expand your territorial boundaries.

The concept of an exclusive franchise territory is widely misunderstood. When a franchisor grants you a territory, he is simply agreeing not to compete with you by selling other franchises or placing company sales representatives in your territory. He does not, and cannot, assure you that other franchisees will not sell to customers in your territory. As independent business owners, franchisees are free to sell to any customers anywhere they like, including customers situated in another franchisee's territory. That freedom applies equally to you as well as to your neighboring franchisees.

13. Trademarks and Symbols

In this section of the UFOC, the franchisor must disclose what steps he has taken to protect the use of the franchise name, trademarks, and symbols. The most obvious step is to register the name or mark with the federal government.

The franchisor must list and describe all logos, slogans, or other commercial symbols associated with the franchise. If there is art work involved in the registered logo or trademark, it should be reproduced in the UFOC.

You should note that franchisors do not always own the exclusive rights to their own trade marks. For example, the trade mark may simply be "applied for," not registered. In that instance, you may run the risk of losing the right to use the trade mark if for some reason the registration should be denied.

On the other hand, there is a lengthy period during which every trade mark is only "applied for," before registration is finally granted. This status is by no means a cause for discounting a franchise opportunity. But a fully registered trade mark is clearly more valuable than one that is still under application. Until the registration has been approved by the U.S. Registrar of Trade Marks, there remains a risk, no matter how small, that the name or mark will not be protected.

Be sure the trade name or trade mark has been registered with the federal government, not just with a city or state agency. Protection of a trade name in the franchisor's home town is useless in your area unless it is backed by federal registration.

14. Patents and Copyrights

Under this heading, the franchisor must list any special patents or copyrights that are "material" to the value of the franchise. If a franchise is supposed to be based on a unique patent or design, look in this section of the UFOC to find the patent number, date, and description. If this information is missing, you might ask yourself whether the product or design is really "unique."

15. Obligation of Franchisee to Participate in the Conduct of the Business

In this section of the disclosure document, the franchisor must state whether the person who buys the franchise must run the business himself, or whether he may hire someone else to manage it for him. Many franchisors sell to "absentee" owners who do not actively participate in the management of the business. If you are investing in a franchise as a "silent" partner, be sure you know whether the franchisor permits absentee partnership. If you intend to hire someone else to manage the business, check to see that the offering circular specifically discloses the franchisor's permission to do so.

16. Restrictions on Goods and Services

It must be disclosed in this section if the franchisee will be limited as to the type of products and services he may sell. For instance, if you are buying a franchise to sell exercise equipment door-to-door, can the franchisor prevent you from selling encyclopedias at the same time? Or if you plan to open a computer store franchise, will you be able to sell copy machines and office furniture as well?

On the surface, this issue may not seem important. But if you already own a convenience store franchise and you're considering a second franchise to sell hot dogs or flavored ice on the premises, you had better be certain the franchises are compatible under the provisions of both franchise agreements.

17. Renewal, Termination, Repurchase, and Assignment

This section of the UFOC spells out the provisions of the franchise agreement dealing with your right to renew the franchise when the contract expires; how the agreement can be involuntarily terminated by either party; whether the franchisor has the right of first refusal to repurchase the franchise; and any restrictions governing assignment of the contract to someone other than the person who originally bought the franchise.

We'll take a closer look at these important issues in Chapter Eleven, when we translate a franchise agreement into plain English.

18. Arrangements with Public Figures

In this section, the franchisor must disclose all the details behind any arrangement to use the name and reputation of a public figure. For instance, let's say you are considering a franchise to start a fast food restaurant with the name of someone called Granny Opry on the sign. Just exactly how is Granny associated with the business? How much is the franchisor paying her to use her name? Unless these facts were disclosed, you might think Granny actually owns the franchising company.

Franchisors sometimes pay famous sports figures, singers, or movie stars to put their names on a franchise offering. Some of these public figures own stock in the franchising corporation, but others have no ownership participation at all.

19. Projected Earnings

This section of the offering circular is used to predict how much you can expect to make in the business. The prediction must be accompanied by the formula used to calculate the projected profits or earnings. No matter how the projections are made, the franchisor must inform you that there is no assurance that you can actually attain such sales levels or earnings.

An earnings projection can only be safely made when the franchisor actually has a large number of outlets that have been open for many years. Even then, the projections should be considered hypothetical, since economic conditions vary greatly from one geographic area to the next.

A far more reliable projection is your own forecast of the economic potential of the business, based partly on information contained in the UFOC, but also on accurate estimates of costs and expenses in your locality. A step-by-step guide to projecting the franchise's potential profits is described in Chapter Nine.

20. *Information Regarding Franchises of the Franchisor*

This section is used to list the number of franchises currently sold and open, their names and addresses, and an estimate of the total number to be granted in the forthcoming year in each state. If a franchisor has problems with franchise terminations, lawsuits, or other disputes, these must be disclosed here.

A new franchisor with no outlets can simply estimate the number to be sold in each state within the twelve months after the effective date of the offering circular.

Before you make a final decision to purchase a franchise, it's wise to contact some of the franchisor's established franchisees. Ask them the questions listed at the end of Chapter Six.

21. *Financial Statements*

A copy of the franchisor's current, audited financial statement *must* be attached to the circular. The rules do not allow any franchisor to substitute an un-audited financial statement of any kind. The financial statement must be audited by a certified public accountant whose official stamp appears on the document, and must be current within six months of the effective date of the offering circular.

22. *Contracts*

A copy of the franchise agreement should be attached to the UFOC. If there are any other related agreements, such as a purchase contract or lease agreement, each of these should be included, as well.

A sample Uniform Franchise Offering Circular based on the specific language prescribed by the FTC appears in Appendix C.

Reading Between the Lines

Although the UFOC is intended to shield you, the prospective investor, against fraudulent business practices, no official regulatory body checks the accuracy of the information. Even in states with strict regulations, the franchise authorities have neither the staff nor the budget to verify the contents of the thousands of UFOCs which cross their desks each year.

In the next chapter, you'll find a list of questions to ask when you evaluate a franchisor's disclosure document.

Chapter Nine

How to Evaluate an Offering Circular

In the last chapter, we examined each section of the Uniform Franchise Offering Circular, or UFOC, and saw what kind of information you can expect to find there. Technically, it's illegal for a franchisor to omit any relevant information, distort or misrepresent some unsavory episode in his past, or disguise a disagreeable aspect of the franchise agreement. But in reality, most UFOCs are prepared by experts who are highly skilled in portraying the franchisor in the most favorable light possible, without stretching or breaching the rules.

It's worth repeating here that nobody but the franchisor actually checks every paragraph of the UFOC to be sure it is accurate or that no vital piece of information has been omitted.

So, to help you sort out the facts, this chapter contains an exhaustive list of questions related to the offering circular. Some of the answers may be found in the franchisor's UFOC; others can only be provided by the franchisor, at your request.

Each set of questions is keyed to one of the sections in the UFOC.

What You Must Know about the Franchisor

1. Franchisor and Any Predecessor

- What other business(es) has the franchisor been associated with in the past?

117

- How long has the franchisor operated a business similar to the proposed franchise outlet?
- What kind of success did the franchisor have in the business?
- What happened to the "predecessor" businesses? Did the franchisor sell them? If so, to whom?

2. Persons Affiliated With the Franchisor

- The UFOC discloses the identity and experience of the principals for the last five years. What are their business backgrounds prior to five years ago?
- Does each principal have the kind of background that justifies his or her present role in the franchise company? For instance, does the finance director have extensive banking or financial experience, and does the training director have solid educational credentials?
- Are the disclosures current and accurate? Are there any major omissions or misrepresentations?

3. Litigation

- The UFOC discloses any relevant criminal or civil actions taken against any of the principals (except in California, where criminal actions are omitted by law). Are the disclosures current and accurate? Have any lawsuits been omitted or misrepresented?
- Only cases involving a franchise law, fraud, embezzlement, or unfair business practices must be disclosed. Are there any other types of litigation pending or in the franchisor's past? If so, what are the nature of the cases?

4. Bankruptcy

- Have any of the principals been involved in a bankruptcy that, for some reason, may have been omitted from the UFOC? If so, what are the particulars? Does the business in question have any bearing on the proposed franchise?
- If a bankruptcy is disclosed, is it largely irrelevant to the franchise business or the principal's qualifications?

118

5. Initial Fee or Other Payment

- Is the franchise fee payable in a lump sum, or may it be paid in installments?
- Where will the initial fee be deposited? In an impoundment or escrow account? In the "general funds" of the franchise company? In the account of a subsidiary or affiliated business?
- Is the initial fee "fully earned" as soon as you pay it? Will you be entitled to a refund if, for some reason, you are unable to open the franchise? If so, how much will be refunded?

6. Other Fees

- Are there any other fees, charges, or royalties besides the franchise royalty? If so, what are they, and how are they payable?
- Does the franchisor charge for site selection assistance? If so, how much is the charge and when must it be paid?
- Does the franchisor charge for marketing consultation or other special assistance? If so, what is the rate and how is it incurred?
- Is there a charge for the training program? If so, how much is it? Will you have to pay for your own travel and living expenses to attend the program?
- Are you required to purchase an opening inventory from the franchisor? If so, what is the wholesale value?

7. Initial Investment

- What is the total amount of all fees, charges, and initial purchases payable to the franchisor?
- What expense items are payable as a lump sum?
- What items may be paid for as they are incurred? To whom must they be paid?
- What is your estimated investment in leases or real estate? In equipment, fixtures, and improvements? In opening inventory purchases? In deposits? In working capital required to sustain the business until it begins to turn a profit?

Use the following form to document the expense items that should be included in the estimated initial investment. If the UFOC omits any of the expense items, ask your franchise sales representative to supply educated estimates *in writing*.

Initial Investment Work Sheet

Item	How Paid	Franchisor's Estimate	Actual Estimate	When Due
Initial Franchise Fee				
Lease				
Fixtures and Improvements				
Insurance				
Equipment and Vehicles				
Initial Inventory				
Business Supplies				
Working Capital				
TOTAL		$_____	$_____	

8. Obligations of Franchisee to Purchase or Lease from Designated Sources

- Will you be obligated to purchase any equipment, supplies, fixtures, or inventory items from a designated supplier? If so, for what reason?
- Are the prices offered by a designated supplier comparable or lower than those offered by any other supplier carrying the same or comparable goods?
- What other benefits are provided by the designated supplier(s)? Availability? Repair-or-replacement warranty?

9. Obligations of Franchisee to Purchase or Lease in Accordance with Specifications or from Approved Suppliers

- Will you be obligated to purchase equipment, supplies, fixtures, or inventory based on minimum technical specifications defined by the franchisor? If so, are the specifications reasonable?
- Are the specifications written in such a manner as to include a number of alternative brands or makes available from a wide range of suppliers? Or are they written so as to limit the type and source?

10. Financing

- Does the franchisor offer any financial assistance? If so, how much of your investment will he finance? At what interest rate?
- Is financing available for any part of your investment, or only for the physical inventory and fixtures?
- Does the franchisor receive any fee or other consideration from the financial source?
- Will the franchisor finance the entire investment over the term of the franchise, and allow you a set income until the loan is fully repaid? In other words, are you really buying a job, rather than a business?

121

11. Obligations of Franchisor

- Specifically what services does the franchisor promise to provide as a normal part of the franchise arrangement (i.e., without additional charge)?
- What services will be provided prior to opening the business? Site selection assistance? Help with negotiating the lease? Help with designing and procuring signage?
- What services will be provided after the business is open? Marketing assistance? Accounting help or advice? Purchasing assistance?

12. Exclusive Territory

- Will you receive a protected territory? Will the franchisor be allowed to sell other franchises or market products within your territory?
- How is the territory defined? Are the geographic boundaries spelled out in detail?
- Is the territory or its size tied to a sales quota or other measure of performance?

13. Trademarks and Symbols

- What steps has the franchisor taken to protect the use of the franchise logo or other trademark?
- Is the logo or trade mark registered with the federal government? Or is it merely registered with some local city, county, or state agency?
- Has the registration been granted, or is it still merely "applied for"?
- Are there any pending conflicts or disputes that might affect your right to use the franchise name, logo, or trade mark in your trading area?

14. Patents and Copyrights

- Are the franchisor's so-called trade secrets protected by patents or copyrights?

- What is the value of any disclosed patents or copyrights to the proposed business?

15. *Obligation of Franchisee to Participate in the Conduct of the Business*

- Do you have the right to hire someone else to actively manage the business?
- Are you contemplating a partnership? If so, does your partner meet all the franchisor's qualifications?
- If the agreement prohibits absentee ownership, what happens if you become permanently disabled during the term of the franchise? Will you lose your investment?

16. *Restrictions on Goods and Services*

- What kinds of business activities, if any, are prohibited by the franchisor? Are the prohibitions reasonable?
- Will you be allowed to own, operate, or participate as an investor in any other type of business besides the franchise? Will you have to sell or discontinue any other businesses you currently own?
- Will entering into the franchise agreement bar you from owning stock in any particular corporation of your choosing? Will you have to sell any stock that you currently own?

17. *Renewal, Termination, Repurchase, and Assignment*

- Will the franchisor have the right to terminate the agreement against your will? If so, on what grounds? Are the stated grounds legal, justifiable, or reasonable?
- On what grounds will you be able to cancel or terminate the agreement?
- Are there restrictions governing your right to sell or otherwise assign the franchise to someone else? If so, are the restrictions legal and reasonable?
- Will the franchisor have the right of first refusal to repurchase the franchise if you decide to sell? If so, on what terms and conditions?

18. Arrangements with Public Figures

- Is a well-known public figure a prominent factor in the likelihood of your success?
- Is the public figure a principal in the business, or tied to a long-term contract?
- If the public figure should back out of the business, how will it affect your business? Is the main value of the franchise derived from the figure's presence?
- Exactly how does the public figure benefit from his or her association with the franchise company?

19. Projected Earnings

- If the franchisor makes any statement regarding projected earnings of the proposed business, what formula was used to calculate the projections?
- Has the franchisor advised you that there is no assurance that you can actually attain the sales or earnings levels disclosed in the UFOC?
- How many outlets were used by the franchisor to produce the projections? Where are they located? How long have they been in business? How long did it take them to begin yielding the sales or earnings used in the projections?
- Are the projections based on average sales or earnings of actual outlets, or are they largely hypothetical (e.g., based on a predicted "trend" or linear regression)?

20. Information Regarding Franchises of the Franchisor

- The names and addresses of established franchisees must be disclosed in the UFOC. Is the list current and accurate?
- When you contacted the franchisees in the list, were they satisfied with their investments? Did they speak favorably about the franchisor? Are their sales or earnings commensurate with the franchisor's statement of projected sales or earnings?
- Do any of the franchisees on the list receive a fee or other consideration for endorsing the franchise operation or otherwise aiding the franchisor to sell new franchises?

21. *Financial Statements*

- Are the franchisor's audited financial statements current, within the last six months?
- What proportion of the franchisor's assets is represented by cash? Are any of the assets intangible?
- If the franchisor is lean on cash, what arrangements exist for backing the company's promises? An approved credit line or letter of credit? An impoundment or escrow fund? Stocks, bonds, or other convertible securities?

Chapter Ten

Grand Designs

How Much Can I Make?

Any sound venture begins with a sound plan. When you sign a franchise agreement, one of the first things your franchisor will do for you is to help you create a business plan. But the most important time to have a financial forecast at your fingertips is before you sign the contract.

Franchisors are prohibited by law from making wild claims of projected sales or earnings. Any projections you do receive are probably unreliable. It's up to you to create a financial forecast for the proposed business, based not on what other franchisees earn in other trading areas, but on what you can realistically do in your own back yard.

One of the important things you can do before making a franchise decision is to construct a business plan to forecast your potential earnings.

The franchise business has many traits in common with a conventional business plan: it predicts revenue from sales, subtracts the cost of goods, budgets expenses, and forecasts cash flow. But as a prospective franchise owner, your forecast will contain at least one extra direct cost: a continuous outgoing flow of franchise royalties.

Before we examine the components of a franchise business plan, let's look at a case history. A bookkeeper, whom I'll call Maxine, decides to open her own accounting service. After researching the franchise market, she settles on a company that, for the sake of illustration, we'll call Book Works, Inc. To determine the viability of the business in her trading area, Maxine conducts a survey of local companies. In a sampling of a hundred business owners in her city, eighteen say they would sign up for Maxine's bookkeeping service.

Encouraged by these results, she sets out to determine just how profitable the franchise might become. Maxine plans to start the business as a sole proprietorship, then incorporate after six months. She estimates that the average revenue she will derive from each client will be $250 per month.

Before she forecasts sales, Maxine talks to the managers of several bookkeeping businesses in her trading area. She discovers that the average monthly enrollment is forty-eight. Maxine divides this number in half to estimate her own first month's sales. In addition, she sets the following sales goals: a five percent increase in sales in each of the first six months after the Grand Opening; a two percent per month increase through the first two years; and a one percent per month increase through the end of the first three years. The following table summarizes Maxine's marketing assumptions:

Average revenue per customer:	$250
First month sales:	24
Sales increase in Months 2-6:	5% per mo.
Sales increase in Months 7-24:	2% per mo.
Sales increase in Months 25-36:	1% per mo.

From the Book Works, Inc. franchise salesman, Maxine learns that, in addition to herself, she will need one employee in the first year, and a second employee hired in the thirteenth month. From the start, she will need a commissioned salesperson to cultivate new business. After checking with other bookkeeping services in the area, Maxine decides to pay each full-time employee a salary of $900 per month. She figures payroll taxes and benefits at twenty percent of salaries. Maxine also decides to pay fifteen percent of gross sales to her commissioned sales representative.

With a little research, she is able to provide accurate estimates for commercial space, supplies, insurance, freight, advertising, and communications in his trading area. In addition to all these expenses, Maxine will have to pay five percent of the gross revenues of the business to her franchisor.

Figure 10-1 shows Maxine's first-year projection. According to this forecast, Maxine's franchise would lose money through the first three months of operation. But in the fourth month, she would begin to recoup her losses and build a profit.

Figure 10-1

Year One

				Month			
	1	2	3	4	5	6	7
Customers	24	25	26	28	29	31	31
Revenues	$6000	6300	6615	6946	7293	7658	7811
Expenses:							
Salaries	2900	2900	2900	2900	2900	2900	2900
Taxes/Ben.	580	580	580	580	580	580	580
Commiss.	900	945	992	1042	1094	1149	1172
Lease	900	900	900	900	900	900	900
Telephone	60	60	60	60	60	60	60
Insurance	300						
Suppl. (.02)	120	126	132	139	146	153	156
Adver. (.12)	720	756	794	833	875	919	937
Janitorial	40	40	40	40	40	40	40
Prof. Svc.	200						200
Misc. (.01)	60	63	66	69	73	77	78
Tot. Exp.	6780	6370	6465	6564	6668	6777	7023
Fran. Royalty	300	315	331	347	365	383	391
Net Profits	$-1080	-385	-180	35	260	497	397

			Month			
	8	9	10	11	12	Totals
Customers	32	33	33	34	34	
Revenues	$7967	8126	8289	8455	8624	90083
Expenses:						
Salaries	2900	2900	2900	2900	2900	34800
Taxes/Ben.	580	580	580	580	580	6960
Commiss.	1195	1219	1243	1268	1294	13512
Lease	900	900	900	900	900	10800
Telephone	60	60	60	60	60	720
Insurance						300
Suppl. (.02)	159	163	166	169	172	1802
Adver. (.12)	956	975	995	1015	1035	10810
Janitorial	40	40	40	40	40	480
Prof. Svc.						400
Misc. (.01)	80	81	83	85	86	901
Tot. Exp.	6870	6918	6967	7016	7067	81485
Fran. Royalty	398	406	414	423	431	4504
Net Profits	$699	802	908	1016	1125	$4094

What does this forecast tell Maxine about the Book Works, Inc. franchise? For one thing, she must be prepared to sustain the business with working capital for at least three months after the Grand Opening. In addition to the costs of equipping and supplying the business prior to opening, she'll need at least another $20,000 to safely weather the difficult startup period before the business begins to turn a profit. For another, she can expect her first-year profits (in addition to the salary she pays herself) to be no greater than about $4000. However, when Maxine extends the forecast for six years, she'll find her total earnings potential in this franchise to be as high $60,000 per year.

This example points out three vital pieces of information that a business plan will tell you: how much working capital you need to start the business, whether or not the franchise can succeed in your market, and how much you can realistically expect to earn.

The Franchise Business Plan

Every franchise business plan has three primary components:

- a prediction of revenues;
- an estimate of expenses;
- a calculation of royalties.

Technically, the franchise royalty is a type of expense. But, because it is directly related to gross revenues and is significantly different from such cost items as lease payments, telephone charges, salaries, etc., it's logical to consider your monthly royalty payment(s) in a separate category.

Since your franchise is largely hypothetical at this point, you'll have to use realistic estimates for most items. A good place to start is by using statistics from other businesses in the same field. If you have an accountant or investment counselor, he or she should be able to provide you with some meaningful averages for income and expenses in the franchise's line of business. You can estimate most of your future expenses yourself simply by doing a little research. To predict revenues, you may need help from your franchisor, or one of his existing franchisees.

Estimating Revenues

Ask your prospective franchisor for sales data of a typical or average outlet. If, for some reason, this data is not available to you, contact one or more of the franchisor's existing franchisees. Consult the list of franchise owners in Section 20 of the UFOC. Find out their average monthly revenues or, if that information is proprietary, the average number of products they sell each month in different price categories. For instance, if you are thinking about a franchise to start a computer store, how many computers does a typical franchisee sell each month? How many printers? How many software programs? What's the average price of an item in each category?

Also find out from an accountant or business broker how much a comparable business in your market sells in an average month. In the example above, what are the average gross monthly sales of a store already established in your city? Do sales fluctuate from one season to another, or do they remain relatively static? What factors seem to affect the sales picture: interest rates, holiday spending?

To estimate your own revenues, start by predicting the number of customers you believe you will have in each month of the year. Be conservative at the start, using a modest figure for starting sales. In Maxine's example, she took a competitor's average monthly sales and divided that figure in half to estimate her starting sales. Each month thereafter, increase the monthly sales figure by a set percentage. For example, you might show a ten percent increase from one month to another, over the first year.

Let's look at an example. Assume you are considering a franchise to rent videotape movies. If it takes you sixty days to procure a site and outfit the store, you can expect to receive no revenues at all in the first two months. But, let's assume that when you open the store in the third month of the fiscal year, you can conservatively expect to rent tapes to 600 customers. If you use a ten percent monthly sales increase, the projection of your first year's revenues would look like the following:

Sales:

	Month					
	1	2	3	4	5	6
Videotape Rentals	$0	0	600	660	726	799

Create a complete monthly sales forecast for the first six years of your proposed franchise. Once you have finished the sales forecast, it's a simple matter to estimate your future revenues. Multiply the number of units you expect to sell in each month by the average selling price.

For instance, let's say that, in your hypothetical video business, the average price of a tape rental will be four dollars. According to your sales prediction, your revenue picture over the first six months would appear as follows:

Revenues:

			Month			
	1	2	3	4	5	6
Videotape Rentals	$0	0	2400	2640	2904	3196

Use your sales prediction to project revenues for all six years of your business plan.

How do you estimate sales if you will have many different products in varying price ranges? The easiest thing to do is to categorize your inventory into three or four manageable ranges. Then compute the average price for a product in each range. Construct a separate sales prediction for each product category and use the average price to project revenues. Add the monthly revenues derived from each category to calculate your total monthly revenue forecast.

For example, let's say that, besides tape rentals, your video business will also rent video cassette recorders, or VCRs. Assume that you expect to rent one VCR for every 20 tapes you rent. Your sales estimate for VCR rentals in the first six months would look like the following:

Sales:

			Month			
	1	2	3	4	5	6
VCR Rentals	$0	0	30	33	36	40

Let's say your price for a VCR rental will be ten dollars. Your total six-month revenue picture would appear as follows:

Revenues:

	Month					
	1	2	3	4	5	6
Videotape Rentals	$0	0	2400	2640	2904	3196
VCR Rentals	$0	0	300	330	360	400
Total Revenues	$0	0	2700	2970	3264	3596

Include a projection for all your primary product categories, using an average price to compute monthly revenues. Be sure to extend the forecast for six years into the future.

Estimating Expenses

The second component of the business plan is expenses. The franchisor's initial investment breakdown in the UFOC lists some of your initial expenses, e.g., opening inventory, fixtures, etc.

But you must determine expenses like monthly lease payments, telephone costs, and salaries firsthand.

● *Wages and Salaries*

Specify a monthly salary amount for yourself as the manager of the business. Then set salaries for any other employees you plan to hire. Compute the total amount you will have to pay out each month for wages and salaries.

For example, let's say you set aside $2,000 per month as your own salary. This figure will allow you to survive during the initial period before the business begins to turn a profit. Let's also assume you plan on hiring two store assistants, each of whom will receive an average of $900 per month in wages. Your total monthly budget for wages and salaries is thus calculated as follows:

Owner/manager	$2000
Assistant #1	900
Assistant #2	900
Total Wages/Sal.	$3800

● Taxes and Benefits

To compute employee taxes and benefits, multiply the total figure for wages and salaries by twenty percent. In practice, this amount may be slightly lower or higher, but for planning purposes, twenty percent is usually a reasonable figure.

In the example, you would estimate your taxes and benefits as follows:

$$\text{Taxes/Ben.} = \$3800 \times .20 = \$760$$

● Monthly Lease Payment

To estimate your monthly lease payment, pretend you have already purchased the franchise, and conduct a search for the perfect site. Consult the classified section of your daily newspaper, or call a commercial real estate agent to get a realistic figure for leasing your prospective site.

If you intend to purchase or build your own site, find out how much your mortgage payments will be at the prevailing interest rate.

Let's assume you decide to lease commercial space for your video store. The site you have in mind is 1800 square feet. If the lessor charges fifty cents per square foot, your monthly lease payment would be computed as follows:

$$\text{Lease Pyt.} = \$1800 \times .50 = \$900$$

● Utility Bill

Contact your local utilities company, and ask them what the average monthly utility bill is for the actual or potential site you selected.

Let's say the power company informs you that in the last year, the previous occupant paid a total of $480 in utility bills. Your monthly utility expenses would be calculated as follows:

$$\text{Utilities} = \$480/12 = \$40$$

● Telephone Charges

Use your local phone company's actual monthly charges as an estimate of your telephone bill. Multiply the basic rate by two, to account for long-distance calls with your franchisor and suppliers.

For instance, let's say that in your area, the phone company's basic charge for a commercial establishment is $30 per month. You would estimate your monthly telephone bill as follows:

$$\text{Telephone} = \$30 \text{ x } 2 = \$60$$

● *Advertising Expenses*

Most businesses budget advertising costs as a percentage of sales. For example, a typical retail business might budget twelve percent of its revenues for advertising. Your franchisor should be able to provide you with realistic guidelines for his line of business. Otherwise, contact your accountant or investment counselor to obtain a general average of what comparable businesses spend on promotion.

First, multiply the percentage by the total predicted revenues for the year; then, divide by twelve to calculate the monthly average.

For example, assume a typical franchise spends an average of eight percent of its gross sales on advertising. If you predict $120,000 in total revenues for the year, your monthly advertising expenses would be estimated as follows:

$$\text{Adver.} = (\$120,000 \text{ x } .08)/12 = \$800$$

● *Professional Services*

Don't forget to include a budget for your accounting or bookkeeping service and your attorney. Use the actual monthly fee quoted by your accountant, and figure the cost of two conferences with your attorney per year.

Assume, for instance, your accountant will charge you $125 per month to maintain your books. Let's say a typical visit to your attorney's office costs you $50. In ten months of each year, your professional services budget will be $125, but in the two months in which you include a conference with your lawyer, the budget will be:

$$\text{Prof. Svcs.} = \$125 + \$50 = \$175$$

● *Commission Expenses*

If your business will use commissioned sales representatives to sell its products or services, estimate your total commission expense

135

by multiplying your figures for sales revenues times the percentage commission.

If all of your sales will be handled by commissioned sales agents, multiply the commission times your total monthly revenues. For example, if you predict $10,000 in sales in a particular month, and your sales representatives earn a five percent commission, you would calculate your commission expenses as follows:

$$\text{Commissions} = \$10,000 \times .05 = \$500$$

If you expect only half of your monthly revenues to be derived from the efforts of commissioned salespeople, your commission expense would be calculated as follows:

$$\text{Commissions} = (\$10,000/2) \times .05 = \$250$$

● *Insurance Premiums*

Contact your insurance agent to find out what your business liability and comprehensive fire/damage insurance premiums will be. Be sure to consult the UFOC or franchise agreement to determine the exact type and amount of coverage you will require.

It is common to make two semi-annual premium payments, so show half of the annual premium paid out in two different months. For example, let's say your business insurance will cost you $300 per year. In the first and seventh months of each year, you would show the following estimated insurance payments:

$$\text{Insurance} = \$300/2 = \$150$$

● *Cost of Supplies*

The cost of supplies, like advertising, can be expressed as a percentage of revenues. In a typical retail business, supplies run from one to two percent of revenues.

Assume, for example, your total predicted revenues for the year will be $120,000. First, multiply that figure by the percentage amount; then, divide by twelve to determine the monthly estimate. If your budget for supplies is two percent, the monthly cost of supplies would be calculated as follows:

$$\text{Supplies} = (\$120,000 \times .02)/12 = \$200$$

136

● *Other Expenses*

Be sure to include any other expense categories that pertain to the proposed business. For instance, if you will be buying and selling products, include the cost of goods and other items, such as freight, delivery, or postage. These costs are normally computed as a percentage of revenues.

The following table illustrates some of the important expense items that might be included in your franchise business plan:

Cost of Goods Sold
Wages/Salaries
Employee Taxes/Benefits
Commissions
Insurance Premiums
Freight/Shipping
Advertising and Promotion
Professional Services
Telephone Charges
Janitorial Service
Supplies
Taxes
Bank Charges
Travel Expenses

Estimating Royalties

The third component of the franchise business plan is the total amount you must send to your franchisor at the end of each month. In most cases, that amount will include both a standard franchise royalty and a co-op advertising royalty.

Franchise royalties are usually determined from gross revenues, not net profits. In other words, the royalty comes off the top, before expenses are deducted.

For example, let's say that in a given month your franchise will generate $10,000 in gross revenues. If your franchise royalty is six percent, your royalty payment would be estimated as follows:

$$Royalty = \$10,000 \times .06 = \$600$$

If your co-op advertising royalty is two percent, this payment would be computed as follows:

$$\text{Co-op Adv.} = \$10,000 \text{ x } .02 = \$200$$

Thus, your total estimated royalty payment for the month would be determined as follows:

Franchise Royalty	$600
Co-op Adv. Royalty	$200
Total Royalty Pyt.	$800

The Profit Forecast

To determine your projected profits from the business, subtract your projected total expenses and royalties from the projected total revenues. In our example of a videotape rental franchise, the profit picture for the first months might appear as follows:

Net Profits

		Month			
1	2	3	4	5	6
Total Revenues	0	0	2700	2970	3264	3596
Total Expenses	32400	3650	3720	3425	3600	3220
Total Royalties	0	0	135	147	163	180
Net Profits	-32400	-3650	-1155	-602	-499	196

In this example, the business begins to make a profit in the sixth month (four months after the doors have opened for business). From this prediction, you would know that you must be able to sustain the business with working capital for at least five months.

Forecasting Cash Flow

Besides projecting your profits or losses at the end of each month, it would be useful to know the business's true cash position at any point. The term "cash position" means how much cash you will actually have on hand at the end of each month. "Cash flow" is a measurement of the positive and negative trends in the cash position of a business.

To project cash flow, add the profit for each month to the profit for the previous month. The business's cash flow is the running total of monthly profits. Express a loss as a negative profit.

In our example of the videotape franchise, the cash flow for the first six months would look like this:

Cash Flow

	Month					
	1	2	3	4	5	6
Net Profits	-32400	-3650	-1155	-602	-499	196
Cash Flow	-32400	-36050	-37205	-37807	-38306	-38110

In this example, cash flow is negative (i.e., a minus figure). The situation gets steadily worse until the sixth month, when the business finally starts to realize a small profit. From here on, the deficit is gradually reduced. If you continued this forecast, you would eventually see the cash flow turn positive, indicating a surplus of cash on hand.

What does this analysis tell you? For one thing, the maximum amount of negative cash flow is $38,306, occurring in the fifth month. After that, the picture starts to improve. In this instance, you would figure your working capital requirement at around $39,000 — enough to keep the business going until it begins to turn a profit.

Figure 10-2 illustrates a three-year forecast for a typical franchise business.

Figure 10-2

Year One

	Month						
	1	2	3	4	5	6	7
Revenues	$36000	39600	43560	47916	52708	57978	63776
Expenses							
Cost of Goods	21600	23760	26136	28750	31625	34787	38266
Salaries	4500	4500	4500	4500	4500	4500	4500
Taxes/Ben.	900	900	900	900	900	900	900
Commiss.	3600	3960	4356	4792	5271	5798	6378
Lease	900	900	900	900	900	900	900
Telephone	60	60	60	60	60	60	60
Insurance	300						
Suppl. (.02)	720	792	871	958	1054	1160	1276
Adver. (.12)	4320	4752	5227	5750	6325	6957	7653
Janitorial	120	120	120	120	120	120	120
Prof. Svc.	250	125	125	125	125	125	250
Misc. (.01)	360	396	436	479	527	580	638
Tot. Exp.	37630	40265	43631	47334	51406	55887	60940
Fran. Royalty	1800	1980	2178	2396	2635	2899	3189
Co-op Adv.	720	792	871	958	1054	1160	1276
Net Profits	-4150	-3437	-3120	-2772	-2388	-1628	1967
Cash Flow	$-4150	-7587	-10707	-13479	-15867	-19462	-17834

	Month					
	8	9	10	11	12	Totals
Revenues	$70154	77169	84886	93375	102712	769834
Expenses:						
Cost of Goods	42092	46302	50932	56025	61627	461901
Salaries	4500	4500	4500	4500	4500	54000
Taxes/Ben.	900	900	900	900	900	10800
Commiss.	7015	7717	8489	9337	10271	76983
Lease	900	900	900	900	900	10800
Telephone	60	60	60	60	60	720
Insurance						300
Suppl. (.02)	1403	1543	1698	1867	2054	15397
Adver. (.12)	8418	9260	10186	11205	12325	92380
Janitorial	120	120	120	120	120	1440
Prof. Svc.	125	125	125	125	125	1750
Misc. (.01)	702	772	849	934	1027	7698
Tot. Exp.	66236	72199	78758	85974	93910	734169
Fran. Royalty	3508	3858	4244	4669	5136	
Co-op Adv.	1403	1543	1698	1867	2054	15397
Net Profits	-993	-431	186	865	1612	-18223

Year Two

			Month				
	13	14	15	16	17	18	19
Revenues	$107848	113240	118902	124847	131089	137644	144526
Expenses:							
Cost of Goods	64709	67944	71341	74908	78654	82586	86716
Salaries	4500	4500	4500	4500	4500	4500	4500
Taxes/Ben.	900	900	900	900	900	900	900
Commiss.	10785	11324	11890	12485	13109	13764	14453
Lease	900	900	900	900	900	900	900
Telephone	60	60	60	60	60	60	60
Insurance	300						
Suppl. (.02)	2157	2265	2378	2497	2622	2753	2891
Adver. (.12)	12942	13589	14268	14982	15731	16517	17343
Janitorial	120	120	120	120	120	120	120
Prof. Svc.	250	125	125	125	125	125	250
Misc. (.01)	1078	1132	1189	1248	1311	1376	1445
Tot. Exp.	98700	102859	107672	112725	118031	123602	129577
Fran. Royalty	5392	5662	5945	6242	6554	6882	7226
Co-op Adv.	2157	2265	2378	2497	2622	2753	2891
Net Profits	1598	2454	2907	3383	3882	4407	4832
Cash Flow	$-16625	-14171	-11264	-7881	-3999	408	5240

			Month			
	20	21	22	23	24	Totals
Revenues	$151752	159340	167307	175672	184456	1716624
Expenses:						
Cost of Goods	91051	95604	100384	105403	110674	1029974
Salaries	4500	4500	4500	4500	4500	54000
Taxes/Ben.	900	900	900	900	900	10800
Commiss.	15175	15934	16731	17567	18446	171662
Lease	900	900	900	900	900	10800
Telephone	60	60	60	60	60	720
Insurance						300
Suppl. (.02)	3035	3187	3346	3513	3689	34332
Adver. (.12)	18210	19121	20077	21081	22135	205995
Janitorial	120	120	120	120	120	1440
Prof. Svc.	125	125	125	125	125	1750
Misc. (.01)	1518	1593	1673	1757	1845	17166
Tot. Exp.	135595	142044	148816	155927	163393	1538940
Fran. Royalty	7588	7967	8365	8784	9223	85831
Co-op Adv.	3035	3187	3346	3513	3689	34332
Net Profits	5535	6142	6780	7449	8151	57520
Cash Flow	$10775	16917	23697	31145	39297	39297

Year Three

				Month			
	25	26	27	28	29	30	31
Revenues	$184456	184456	184456	184456	184456	184456	184456
Expenses:							
Cost of Goods	110674	110674	110674	110674	110674	110674	110674
Salaries	4500	4500	4500	4500	4500	4500	4500
Taxes/Ben.	900	900	900	900	900	900	900
Commiss.	18446	18446	18446	18446	18446	18446	18446
Lease	900	900	900	900	900	900	900
Telephone	60	60	60	60	60	60	60
Insurance	300						
Suppl. (.02)	3689	3689	3689	3689	3689	3689	3689
Adver. (.12)	22135	22135	22135	22135	22135	22135	22135
Janitorial	120	120	120	120	120	120	120
Prof. Svc.	250	125	125	125	125	125	250
Misc. (.01)	1845	1845	1845	1845	1845	1845	1845
Tot. Exp.	163818	163393	163393	163393	163393	163393	163518
Fran. Royalty	9223	9223	9223	9223	9223	9223	9223
Co-op Adv.	3689	3689	3689	3689	3689	3689	3689
Net Profits	7726	8151	8151	8151	8151	8151	8026
Cash Flow	$47023	55175	63326	71478	79629	87781	95807

			Month			
	32	33	34	35	36	Totals
Revenues	$184456	184456	184456	184456	184456	2213472
Expenses:						
Cost of Goods	110674	110674	110674	110674	110674	1328083
Salaries	4500	4500	4500	4500	4500	54000
Taxes/Ben.	900	900	900	900	900	10800
Commiss.	18446	18446	18446	18446	18446	221347
Lease	900	900	900	900	900	10800
Telephone	60	60	60	60	60	720
Insurance						300
Suppl. (.02)	3689	3689	3689	3689	3689	44269
Adver. (.12)	22135	22135	22135	22135	22135	265617
Janitorial	120	120	120	120	120	1440
Prof. Svc.	125	125	125	125	125	1750
Misc. (.01)	1845	1845	1845	1845	1845	22135
Tot. Exp.	163393	163393	163393	163393	163393	1961261
Fran. Royalty	9223	9223	9223	9223	9223	110674
Co-op Adv.	3689	3689	3689	3689	3689	44269
Net Profits	8151	8151	8151	8151	8151	97268
Cash Flow	$103959	112110	120262	128413	136565	136565

Interpreting the Forecast

After you have projected your proposed franchise's future profits and cash flows, you will be in possession of some very useful information. For one thing, you will have a realistic snapshot of how well this type of business can do in your own market. For another, you will have a clear view of how much you can expect to earn. You'll also know how much working capital you will need to keep the business going until it becomes profitable. Finally, the franchise business plan will provide you with a basis for obtaining financial assistance when and if you need it.

The work sheets on the following pages will help you organize information about revenues and expenses, and construct a meaningful financial forecast for any franchise you are considering. Before you start, make a separate photocopy of each work sheet for every year of your forecast. Use the first sheet to record your estimates for the first six months of each fiscal year, and the second sheet for months seven through twelve. The last sheet is used to record the annual totals.

Year

Month	1	2	3	4	5	6
Net Sales	___	___	___	___	___	___
Cost of Goods	___	___	___	___	___	___
Total Revenues	___	___	___	___	___	___
Salaries	___	___	___	___	___	___
Taxes/Ben.	___	___	___	___	___	___
Commissions	___	___	___	___	___	___
Space Lease	___	___	___	___	___	___
Supplies	___	___	___	___	___	___
Equipment	___	___	___	___	___	___
Insurance	___	___	___	___	___	___
Advertising	___	___	___	___	___	___
Legal/Acct.	___	___	___	___	___	___
Communications	___	___	___	___	___	___
___	___	___	___	___	___	___
___	___	___	___	___	___	___
___	___	___	___	___	___	___
___	___	___	___	___	___	___
Royalty Pyt.	___	___	___	___	___	___
Co-op Ad Fund	___	___	___	___	___	___
___	___	___	___	___	___	___
Tot. Oper. Exp.	___	___	___	___	___	___
Pre-tax Profit	___	___	___	___	___	___
Income Taxes	___	___	___	___	___	___
Net Income	___	___	___	___	___	___

Year						
Month	7	8	9	10	11	12
Net Sales	___	___	___	___	___	___
Cost of Goods	___	___	___	___	___	___
Total Revenues	___	___	___	___	___	___
Salaries	___	___	___	___	___	___
Taxes/Ben.	___	___	___	___	___	___
Commissions	___	___	___	___	___	___
Space Lease	___	___	___	___	___	___
Supplies	___	___	___	___	___	___
Equipment	___	___	___	___	___	___
Insurance	___	___	___	___	___	___
Advertising	___	___	___	___	___	___
Legal/Acct.	___	___	___	___	___	___
Communications	___	___	___	___	___	___
___	___	___	___	___	___	___
___	___	___	___	___	___	___
___	___	___	___	___	___	___
___	___	___	___	___	___	___
Royalty Pyt.	___	___	___	___	___	___
Co-op Ad Fund	___	___	___	___	___	___
___	___	___	___	___	___	___
Tot. Oper. Exp.	___	___	___	___	___	___
Pre-tax Profit	___	___	___	___	___	___
Income Taxes	___	___	___	___	___	___
Net Income	___	___	___	___	___	___

Annual Totals

Year _____

	Total	%
Net Sales	____	1.00
Cost of Goods	____	·__
Total Revenues	____	·__
Salaries	____	·__
Taxes/Ben.	____	·__
Commissions	____	·__
Space Lease	____	·__
Supplies	____	·__
Equipment	____	·__
Insurance	____	·__
Advertising	____	·__
Legal/Acct.	____	·__
Communications	____	·__
_____	____	·__
_____	____	·__
_____	____	·__
_____	____	·__
Royalty Pyt.	____	·__
Co-op Ad Fund	____	·__
Tot. Oper. Exp.	____	·__
Pre-tax Profit	____	
Income Taxes	____	
Net Income	____	

Chapter Eleven

A Meeting of Minds

The Franchise Agreement

When Michael R. visited the franchise headquarters of Golden Future Computer Centers, he was so dazzled by what he saw that he insisted on signing a contract on the spot. The franchisor's legal department had sent Michael a copy of the UFOC and franchise agreement two weeks before he arrived, fulfilling the company's obligation to place the disclosures in the hands of the prospective franchisee at least ten business days prior to signing. Michael had read the documents and shared them with his attorney, who, knowing little about franchising, browsed through them in two hours and rendered his general approval.

Neither Michael nor his attorney paid much attention to two seemingly minor points in the contract. The first was a statement to the effect that Michael, as the franchisee, had read the agreement in its entirety and understood and accepted all its terms, conditions, and covenants as being "reasonable and necessary." The second was a provision that in the event of Michael's disability or death, no heirs or successors could acquire any rights or interests in the franchise. In other words, if Michael should become permanently disabled or die, his wife, children, or any other heirs would lose all ownership in the business.

147

Clearly, this was not what Michael intended when he set out to start his own business. Yet, when he suffered a heart attack seven years later, the company moved in quickly and took over the business.

Later in court, Michael's attorneys contended that the franchisor's sales representatives had not adequately explained this provision to Michael prior to his signing the agreement. But when Michael executed the franchise contract, he was also signing an acknowledgment that he fully understood and agreed with every word.

What his franchisor had described as a "simple formality" ended up costing Michael and his heirs his life's work and legacy. You should remember that a franchisor's attorneys are usually experts in drafting franchise agreements, most of which are designed to produce maximum leverage for the franchisor. In contrast, your legal counsel is more likely to be an independent attorney with little experience in franchise contracts or disputes.

Knowing how a franchise contract is drafted and what ramifications may result from each provision is one of the most valuable assets you can bring to the bargaining table.

There are almost as many different franchise agreements as there are franchise businesses, but there are many elements common to all good franchise contracts. The basic agreement has fifteen parts. Each defines one of the important relationships between franchisor and franchisee.

1. Grant of Franchise

You might find this part of the contract in the "preambles." The preamble section summarizes the reason for the contract and states the mutual objectives of the parties signing it. However, it may also contain some legal language that may have an enormous bearing on your rights as a franchisee.

For example, the contract may contain a statement that you have read the Uniform Franchise Offering Circular and franchise agreement in their entirety, and accept all the terms, provisions, and covenants as being "reasonable and necessary." If you were the franchisor, you would certainly want this acknowledgment clearly stated and agreed to in writing. A franchisee involved in a legal dispute often claims that the franchisor failed to adequately explain all the details of the franchise contract. But as a prospective franchisee, be sure you really have read every word of the agreement, and understand what each sentence means.

When you sign the franchise agreement, you may also be signing an oath that could let your franchisor off the hook in the event of a future dispute over some aspect of the agreement.

The grant of franchise may also include a precisely defined territory. For example, the contract might state, "FRANCHISOR agrees that it will not compete with FRANCHISEE in the designated territory, nor establish another franchise therein."

In other words, the franchisor will not sell products to customers in your territory, or sell a franchise to someone else inside your territory. If a franchisor grants you a protected territory, he cannot restrain you from selling to customers outside its boundaries. The territory constrains the franchisor, not the franchisee.

2. Trademarks and Identity

This section of the agreement states who owns the trade name, trademarks, and logos associated with the franchise, and gives you a license to use them. The owner is usually the franchisor himself, or, possibly, a public figure affiliated with the franchisor. The agreement also obligates you to protect the franchisor's trademarks against infringement by others. In addition, you agree to use the trademarks only in a manner approved by the franchisor.

In plain English, that means the franchisor controls the business name and logo. For instance, he may let you order pens with the business name imprinted on the side, but he might want to forbid you from printing up girlie calendars featuring the company logo.

If you come across any unauthorized use of the trademarks by someone else, you are bound to notify the franchisor at once. For example, let's say you buy a franchise which uses the trade name "Go-Video." One day, you come across a competitor using the name "Go-Go Video." It's your duty to call the franchisor and report this obvious infringement. A registered trademark has no value unless its exclusivity is protected by those who are licensed to use it.

The agreement also usually obligates you to discontinue using the trademarks if the franchisor loses his own rights to them.

Simply acquiring the rights to a trademark through a franchise agreement may not give you the right to use it in your area. A franchisor secures federal registration of a trade name or mark by being the first one to implement it in interstate commerce. But someone else might already have the right to use the same name or trademark in a city, county, or state where the franchisor has not previously done business. As a result, you could actually end up buying a franchise and not being able to use the franchise name in your area.

Even though you obtain a license to use the franchisor's trademarks, you must obtain a business name permit (often called a DBA, for "doing business as") before you can use the name in your own business. A state, county, or city agency is usually responsible for dispensing these permits. The idea is to assure that competing businesses don't use the same name in the same trading area. If someone else has already acquired a permit to use the same or a similar name as your franchise, the trademark license may be a hollow commodity. Thus, investigate your right to use the franchise trademarks in your area *before* you sign the franchise agreement.

Assume, for example, that you buy a franchise which uses the trade name "Rocket Messenger." When you go to City Hall to take out a business name permit, you discover to your chagrin that another company in town already has the rights to that name. As a result, the permit is denied. Unfortunately, your franchisor's co-op advertising will be of very little value to you if you can't use the advertised name. You might be able to convince the other business to change its name, but not without compensation.

3. Relationships of the Parties

A franchisee is an independent business owner who contracts with a franchisor for the services and benefits specified in the agreement. As such, neither party may incur debts on the other's behalf. The franchise agreement does not make either party a subsidiary or affiliate of the other. Each is liable for his own taxes, debts, and contracts.

In plain English, your franchisor is not liable for your behavior. For example, if a customer trips on a freshly waxed floor and cracks a vertebra, you — not your franchisor — will be held liable. Likewise, if you cheat on your tax returns, it's your problem, not your franchisor's.

4. Fees and Payments

In this section, you agree to pay the initial franchise fee. The fee may be due on signing the agreement, or it may be payable in installments. As a franchisee, you also agree to pay the specified royalty, and to make sure it is paid on time each month. If your royalty payments are late, the agreement may stipulate interest or penalties.

If your franchisor has a co-op advertising fund, your monthly advertising royalty should also be stated in this section of the agreement.

If your franchisor will also be one of your vendors, e.g., a product distributor or equipment supplier, the agreement may give the franchisor the right to apply your royalty payments against any other amounts you may owe. For example, the contract may state something like, "FRANCHISOR shall have sole discretion to apply any payments by FRANCHISEE to any past-due indebtedness of FRANCHISEE to FRANCHISOR."

Let's say you buy a franchise to open a restaurant, and your franchisor happens to sell restaurant fixtures and supplies. Assume you buy these items from the franchisor on credit. Later on, when your restaurant opens, you mail in your first royalty check. To your consternation, the franchisor applies the royalty payment against the amount you owe for fixtures and supplies. As a result, your royalty remains unpaid and begins to accrue penalties.

If a provision like this appears in a franchise agreement, be sure your franchisor gives you a full and clear explanation before you sign. Ask for examples of how the provision might apply in your case.

5. Training and Guidance

In most franchise agreements, the franchisor agrees to provide a training program of a set length, e.g., two weeks. The agreement may require you to pay for your own travel and living costs to attend the training program. In addition, there may be a surcharge for additional attendees, such as a partner or manager. If these points are unclear in the agreement, ask the franchisor to clarify them.

The franchisor may also agree to provide other guidance and services, such as ongoing advice and consultation, a franchise manual, or assistance in selecting a site for your business.

Most franchise agreements state that the operating manual is loaned, not given or sold, to the franchisee. The logic is that the manual contains the franchisor's success secrets and, therefore, is accessible to you only during the term of your franchise. When your franchise expires, so does your access to the trade secrets. Hence, you usually must agree to return the manual and all updates, bulletins, and revisions to the franchisor if and when you and your franchisor part ways.

6. Operating System

In this section, you agree to abide by the franchisor's operating policies and performance standards. The agreement may also obligate you to help keep them secret.

You might also find one or more of the following provisions:

a. As a franchisee, you will be prevented from using the franchise business system in any other business.

b. You must keep every aspect of the business secret.

c. Neither you nor your employees may copy the franchise manual or any other written communication from the company.

d. Employees of your franchise must sign oaths of confidentiality.

In other words, you can't buy the franchise, learn all its success secrets, and then sell those secrets to someone else. Nor can you start another business under a different name using the methods and techniques you learned from the franchisor.

These are reasonable precautions designed to protect the value of the franchise. They work in your favor, as well as your franchisor's. Your franchisor's secrets, methods, and techniques are your competitive edge; the moment they fail to remain secret, your franchise instantly loses value.

7. Development and Improvement

The franchise agreement usually requires you to lease and develop your outlet within a specified period, e.g., ninety days. You also agree to purchase the equipment, fixtures, signs, and inventory you need to open the business. The franchisor may agree to help out with Grand Opening activities, or to send a field representative to assist you in developing the outlet.

Often, a franchise agreement is struck before there is even a site for the proposed outlet. If that's the case, be sure the deadline for opening the business gives you enough time to evaluate potential sites, negotiate a lease, and secure financing. In addition, you'll have to obtain business licenses, signs, and inventory. Negotiate for more time, if you think you really need it. Providing your request is reasonable, the franchisor should be moderately flexible on this issue.

152

For example, let's say you are considering a franchise to open a car rental agency, and the franchise agreement calls for you to open for business within sixty days. You will need a business loan to finance the outlet. You know a bank that will lend you the money, but it will take ninety days to process the loan application. Considering all the other things you must accomplish before opening — obtaining a site, ordering vehicles, hiring employees, etc. — you ask your franchisor to extend the deadline to 120 days. If you are serious about buying the franchise, the franchisor will probably amend the agreement to give you the time you need. But if you ask for nine months or a year, most likely the negotiations will fall apart.

From the franchisor's point of view, the deadline for developing the outlet encourages rapid market penetration in a new area. He doesn't want the territory sitting idle once he has awarded a franchise. But as a prospective franchisee, you want the deadline to be realistic in the light of business conditions in your locality.

Besides placing a deadline on opening the outlet, the franchise agreement should state exactly who selects the site. Will the franchisor determine the best location for your business? Or will he merely offer advice? Will you be responsible for picking the site? Or will a third party, such as a property developer or realtor, decide where the business will be located?

As a franchisee, you want the benefit of the franchisor's experience in the business. He knows the right customer demographics, traffic flow, and environment for the outlet. On the other hand, you might have a better grasp of the local economic conditions.

Some franchisors who say they will select a site actually contract with a commercial realtor or property manager to recommend an appropriate site. Indeed, a realtor has ready access to suitable properties. But does he have your best interests at heart? Will he focus on sites offering the highest commission or on some other self-serving benefit?

These issues may seem minor at the time, but they can easily become major problems after the franchise agreement is signed. For example, let's say you select your own site for the outlet. A few months later, the business falls into adverse financial straits. You blame your franchisor for failing to provide ongoing assistance, as promised. But, to your aggravation, the franchisor argues that your business is failing only because you selected the wrong site.

Now consider the opposite side of that coin. Let's assume you're the franchisor. As part of your program, you select the site for your franchisee's outlet. Despite your best efforts, one of your franchises fails, plagued by mismanagement and neglect. But in court, the franchisee's attorneys claim the problem was that you picked a bad location.

The solution is to make sure there's a meeting of minds before any site is selected. Both franchisor and franchisee should approve the site in writing before a lease is signed.

8. Image and Conduct

This section of the agreement spells out your obligations to maintain the franchisor's presumably high standards of image and conduct. For example, you might be obligated to keep the outlet clean and orderly, comply with certain merchandising standards, maintain adequate insurance coverage, and obey all laws and ordinances which apply to the business.

On the surface, these guidelines seem innocuous enough. After all, uniformity *is* the primary component in franchise success, and without the ability to enforce uniform standards, the whole idea of franchising dissipates. Ironically, these very contract provisions relating to quality, cleanliness, and appearance are the classic parents of franchise dispute, disorder, and distress.

Why? Because a franchisor's attorney sometimes devises these conditions as a "safety valve" for ridding the organization of an unruly franchisee. The list of standards may be so inclusive that practically any outlet could be found in violation at any given time.

A crooked poster, a wrinkled menu, a smudged uniform, or an unemptied ashtray could technically put you in default of the franchise agreement. In the past, some franchisors have used tiny spots on window panes, gum wrappers on restroom floors, and salt granules on table tops as excuses for forcefully terminating a franchise.

Over the last several decades, hundreds of franchise disputes have centered on this volatile issue, prompting several states to pass legislation granting additional rights to franchisees. Today, a franchisor must allow a franchisee a reasonable opportunity to correct the default. In some states, the law prohibits *any* involuntary termination of a franchise for a default in the franchisor's standards of image and cleanliness.

Besides mandatory standards, the agreement may also spell out how much insurance you must carry. Be certain your insurance carrier or agent understands your obligations and can comply exactly. Many carriers simply do not insure franchises at all. The agreement usually requires the franchisor to be named as an additional insured party on your business liability policy.

9. Advertising and Marketing

Most franchise agreements require you to use only advertising materials and media which were developed or approved by the franchisor. As a result, you will probably be limited as to the type of advertising programs you may conduct. For instance, the agreement may give the franchisor the right to prohibit you from using such items as pens, paper weights, or calendars with naked ladies to promote your franchise.

You might find this restriction vaguely cloaked in such generalized language as "materials which the franchisor, in its sole discretion, may deem unsuitable." Ask the franchisor exactly what kinds of advertising materials he considers "unsuitable." Besides the ones he *doesn't* want you to use, what advertising media *are* approved for promoting your business? Are those media readily available in your locality? Are they as effective in your market as in others? Are they as affordable?

For example, let's say you are considering a franchise to operate a financial counseling business. Based on his past success, the franchisor requires you to spend most of your advertising budget on radio and television ads. But what if those media are two or three times more costly in your market than in most others? Does the franchisor have an alternative advertising plan?

10. Reports and Audits

The typical franchise agreement requires you to maintain all the books and records required to document your tax liability and determine your royalty payments. In addition, you may have to prepare periodic financial statements and submit copies to your franchisor.

The agreement may also give the franchisor the right to audit your records at any time. From his point of view, it's important to be able to verify the accuracy of royalty payments. The right to conduct an audit is an integral and necessary safeguard against cheating.

As a prospective franchisee, you should ask: Who pays for the audit? It's one thing to demand an accounting, another to make you

155

bear the cost. An audit by a public accounting firm is expensive. A good compromise is for the franchisor to pay the cost unless the audit uncovers a significant discrepancy or problem. The amount of the discrepancy should be stated in the franchise agreement. Here's an example:

> If as a result of the audit a discrepancy in excess of three and one half percent (3½%) is found to exist, then FRANCHISEE shall pay all costs incurred in connection with the audit.

This kind of arrangement protects both parties. It protects the franchisor against the possibility of cheating by franchisees, and it protects you against frivolous and costly audits.

11. Assignment of the Franchise

Most franchise agreements will restrict your ability to sell your franchise to someone else. If for some reason you decide to sell the business, the buyer may have to meet with the franchisor's approval. The term most often used in a franchise agreement is "assignment" of the franchise. Assignment means any change in ownership, whether by sale or transfer. When you sell, or otherwise transfer ownership of the business, the new owner is thus the "assignee."

Who are the potential assignees of your franchise? Besides someone who buys the business, your heirs or beneficiaries might also become assignees, in the event of your death or disability. So, when a franchisor says your franchise may not be assigned without his approval, the right of your heirs to inherit the business may be at stake.

The franchisor may also reserve the "right of first refusal" to buy your franchise. This means that if you decide to sell the business, or if you should pass away while you own it, the franchisor is first in line to purchase the franchise. But he also has the right to refuse, clearing the way for a sale to someone else.

If your franchisor has the right of first refusal, you must offer it for sale to him before anyone else. He will have the right to buy the business for the same price and on the same conditions as any other buyer. For example, let's say you already own a franchise, and someone offers you $300,000 for your business. Before you can accept the offer, you must give the franchisor an opportunity to buy the franchise at the same price. If the franchisor accepts, you have no choice but to sell the business to him for $300,000. If he declines, you may proceed with the sale to the original buyer — assuming, of course, he meets your franchisor's approval.

It's not difficult to understand why a franchisor wants to have control over the sale of one of its franchises. Primarily, he wants to protect the franchise from falling into the hands of an unqualified party. After all, his company invests a great deal of time, effort, and money to recruit, train, and establish a suitable franchisee. He can hardly afford to have the business end up in the possession of someone who does not meet the standard qualifications of other franchisees.

Be sure you understand your franchisor's rights regarding assignment of the franchise. Those rights invariably restrict yours. For example, if you become disabled, the agreement may require you to sell or transfer the business to someone else. If you fail to assign the franchise within a designated period, your franchisor may have the right to take it from you without your permission.

The provisions for assignment also affect franchises operated as a corporation. A franchisor grants franchises to individuals, based on their personal traits — not to business entities such as corporations. When you incorporate, technically you are assigning the franchise to another party.

The agreement may place certain restrictions on your ability to assign your franchise to a corporation:

a. As the franchisee, you must remain in control of the business, i.e., as the majority stockholder and chief executive of the corporation.

b. You must disclose the names of all directors, stockholders, and officers to the franchisor.

c. The franchisor may have the right to approve any sale or transfer of the stock.

12. Renewal

Most, but not all, franchises have a definite term. In other words, they expire after a certain period of time, and must be renewed. Five percent of the franchise agreements currently in force do not have a definite term, meaning that the franchisee's rights never expire. About half of all franchise agreements in use today have a term of ten years.

The agreement usually gives you the right to renew the franchise for another term as the end of the first term approaches. However, to renew the franchise you must usually sign a new agreement. That agreement may not be the same as the one you originally signed. In this way, franchisors can periodically "update" their franchise programs, by changing the terms and conditions of the franchise agreements as they come up for renewal.

The shorter the term, the more flexibility the franchisor has to make changes in its organization. On the other hand, as a prospective franchisee making a substantial investment in the franchise, you deserve the opportunity to reap just rewards. It may take a business as long as three years to begin turning a profit. If the franchise term is only five years, you hardly have enough time to realize a decent return.

13. Termination

This section of the agreement spells out the rights of both parties to terminate the contract. For example, if you abandon the business, or are convicted of a felony, the franchisor may have the right to take the franchise from you. On the other hand, you may have the right to terminate the contract if the franchisor fails to fulfill his obligations.

Many franchise agreements say that a franchisor can terminate the franchise unilaterally if you declare bankruptcy. However, you should be aware that, under the Federal Bankruptcy Law, bankruptcy alone may not be used as an excuse to repossess your franchise. But if you fail to keep the doors open for business, you risk losing your investment for "abandoning the franchise."

State laws vary regarding the franchisor's right to terminate a franchise agreement. *No matter what your franchise agreement says, the local statute or ordinance is binding on your franchisor.* For example, the California Franchise Investment Protection Law forbids franchisors from terminating an agreement without "good cause." Good cause is defined as a failure to provide due notice regarding a dispute or default, or a failure to allow the franchisee ample opportunity to correct such a dispute or default. If you live in Mississippi, and a franchisor terminates the agreement, he must be prepared to repurchase your inventory of goods.

For example, let's say you buy a franchise to sell a product which is exclusively distributed by your franchisor. You order a large opening inventory of products. When the shipment arrives, your franchisor can't suddenly cancel the agreement and stick you with a warehouse full of goods. This law helps to assure that franchisors are genuinely interested in your personal success, not merely in taking advantage of you as a captive customer.

14. Obligations Upon Termination or Expiration

If, for any reason, you and your franchisor should part ways, this section of the agreement spells out your obligations. For example, you may be required to return the franchise manual and cease using any of the franchisor's trademarks. You might also have to give up your business phone number.

Most agreements contain a "covenant not to compete." In the covenant, you pledge not to compete with the franchisor in the same business after the agreement expires or is terminated. You should be aware that such covenants are not valid in some states, including California, the largest franchise market.

15. Enforcement and Construction

Every good agreement has a morass of perplexing legal terminology dealing with issues like "severability," "substitution," "governing law," and "binding effect."

The "severability" clause assures that the contract remains in force though part of the agreement may happen to be struck down in court. For example, let's say you sign a franchise agreement which contains a covenant not to compete. Later, a court rules that all such covenants are unenforceable in your state. Even though this part of your franchise agreement may be unenforceable, the rest of the agreement remains in full force and effect.

A "substitution" clause simply means that if the local law is different from any provision in the agreement, that law is automatically substituted for the offending provision. Assume, for instance, that you sign a franchise agreement which states that to renew the contract, you must notify the franchisor at least one year before the expiration date. However, the law in your state allows you to wait sixty days before the contract expires to make up your mind. In this case, the sixty-day requirement mandated by law is automatically substituted for the one-year requirement in the agreement.

The "governing law" clause stipulates which state's laws will be used to interpret the agreement in the event of a dispute. Almost invariably, this is the state in which the franchisor is headquartered.

The basic parts of a franchise agreement are illustrated in the sample franchise agreement in Appendix B. As you evaluate an agreement, you should seek the assistance of an attorney with ample franchise experience. If your own attorney doesn't have the appropriate background, ask him or her to recommend a lawyer or firm that has more experience handling franchise cases.

Remember that the franchisor's lawyers draft the contract to provide maximum advantage for the franchisor, but cloaked in innocent-sounding verbiage. An agreement between a franchisor and franchisee falls under special rules and interpretations that are different from other types of contracts.

In the next chapter, you'll find a list to help you interpret, understand, and evaluate a franchise agreement.

Chapter Twelve

How to Evaluate
a Franchise Agreement

In the last chapter, we examined the important sections of a franchise agreement and learned how its provisions affect your rights as a franchisee. This chapter contains an exhaustive checklist for evaluating a franchise agreement.

Each set of questions is keyed to one of the main sections of a typical franchise agreement. There are many different forms of agreements, and you may find some sections ordered differently, or combined with other sections.

As you study the agreement, try to answer the questions that apply in this checklist. If you can't find the answer in the agreement, or if the answer isn't clear, circle the question on the checklist. When you sit down at the negotiating table prior to signing the agreement, ask the franchisor or his representative to answer or clarify each question you circled.

1. Grant of Franchise

- Have you read the agreement in its entirety?
- Do you understand and accept all the terms, provisions, and covenants?
- Do you consider them reasonable and necessary to the success of the business?

161

- Does the agreement provide you with a specified territory?
- Is the territory precisely defined according to generally accepted geographic boundaries?
- Does your franchisor agree not to compete within the specified territory?
- Does the agreement stipulate that no other franchisor will sell any franchises to others in your territory?
- Does the agreement attempt to restrict you from selling your goods or services to customers outside your territory?
- Are your rights to the territory, or its size, tied to your fiscal performance or a sales quota?
- What sub-franchising rights, if any, will you have within the territory?
- Is the term of the franchise at least ten years, or enough time to allow you to realize a decent return after enduring the difficult startup years?

2. Trademarks and Identity

- Does the franchisor own the trademarks associated with the franchise business?
- Are the trademarks owned by or associated with a public figure? If the answer to the previous question is "yes," is the public figure a principal in the franchising company, or merely a promotional spokesperson?
- Does the franchisor agree to protect the use of the trademarks against unlawful infringement by others?
- Is the trademark or logo registered with the federal government, or merely with some local state, county, or municipal agency?
- Is the trademark or logo registered, or is it merely "applied for"?
- Are there any trade names or marks in use by others in your trading area similar to the franchise trademark, or likely to cause confusion with the franchise trademark?
- Does any one else in your local jurisdiction have the prior right to use the same trademark as the franchise through a fictitious name permit or "dba"?

3. Relationship of the Parties

- Does the franchise agreement recognize that you are an independent contractor, not an agent, employee, or subsidiary of the franchisor?
- Does the agreement acknowledge that you are liable for your own debts, liabilities, and taxes, and that you are not liable for any debts, liabilities, or taxes incurred by the franchisor?
- If your franchisor should happen to be sued for some act or policy for which it is solely responsible, will you be indemnified and held free of blame?

4. Fees and Payments

- Is the amount of the franchise fee clearly stipulated, to the exact penny?
- Is the time at which the franchise fee is due clearly stated?
- Is the franchise royalty clearly stipulated to the exact percentage point or fraction of a percent?
- Is the day of the month on which the royalty is due clearly stated?
- Is the amount of any co-op advertising contribution clearly stated?
- Does the agreement provide for the royalty or co-op ad contribution to be increased unilaterally by the franchisor in the future?
- Does the franchisor have the right to apply your royalty payments to other accounts, such as amounts you owe for fixtures, supplies, or inventory?

5. Training and Guidance

- Does the franchisor provide a training program?
- What is the length of the program?
- Where is the program held?
- Are you obligated to pay for your own travel and living expenses while attending the training program?
- Will the franchisor provide you with a franchise manual?

- What type of ongoing assistance is your franchisor obligated to provide?
- Does the agreement stipulate the number and frequency of visits by a representative of the franchise company?
- Will you have the right to seek guidance from the franchisor any time you need it, or only when a representative makes one of his periodic visits?

6. Operating Systems

- What steps are you obligated to take to protect the franchisor's trade secrets?
- Does the agreement require you to make your employees sign a contract containing an oath of secrecy and a covenant not to compete?
- Will you be prohibited from conducting any other business activity while you own the franchise?
- What other kinds of businesses or activities are permitted?

7. Development and Improvement

- Are you required to lease a site within a certain period? If so, is the length reasonable, in light of local business, real estate, and regulatory conditions?
- Are you required to complete all improvements and inventory purchases within a specified period?
- What are the penalties if you fail to meet the time restrictions?
- Will your franchisor provide assistance in selecting the best site for the business?
- If so, can the franchisor delegate this obligation to a local realtor or leasing agent without your permission?
- Will a representative of the franchise company personally assist you in obtaining a site, or will the company simply hand you a site selection kit?
- If you must select a site on your own, what kind of reference materials, demographics, or other tools will the franchisor provide?
- Will the franchisor help you negotiate a favorable lease?

- Does the agreement stipulate the length of the lease, or any other terms or conditions?
- If, for some reason, you fail to meet your obligations to open the outlet within a specified period, and the franchisor has the right to cancel, will at least half of your franchise fee be refunded?

8. Image and Conduct

- Are the franchisor's mandatory operating standards reasonable and necessary?
- Will the franchisor have the right to terminate the agreement unilaterally, in the event of a default?
- Has the franchisor provided you with a written list containing examples of specific defaults?
- Does your state have laws giving you additional rights as a franchisee?
- If so, has the franchisor informed you that the portions of the agreement relating to defaults in operating standards may be invalid?
- What is the penalty for a default?
- How long will you have to cure an alleged default after receiving a notice from the franchisor?
- Is the length of time reasonable?
- Does the agreement stipulate the type and amount of business liability or other insurance you must carry?
- Is the stipulated insurance available in your area?
- If the answer is "yes," will you be able to afford the premiums?

9. Advertising and Marketing

- Does the agreement provide for a co-op ad fund?
- Is the amount of your advertising royalty clearly defined as either a set amount or percentage?
- Can the amount of your advertising royalty be increased by the franchisor without your consent?
- Does the agreement limit you as to the type of advertising media you may use to promote the business?

- What advertising assistance will the franchisor provide in your local area?
- Does the agreement obligate the franchisor to conduct a certain number or type of advertising efforts?
- Will the franchisor provide Grand Opening assistance?

10. *Reports and Audits*

- Does the agreement permit the franchisor to audit your books and records at any time without notice?
- Does the agreement clearly define the types of reports you must submit periodically?
- Are the franchisor's books available for your inspection at the principal business address?
- If the franchisor conducts an audit of your records, will you be obligated to pay all the costs?
- If there is a dispute or discrepancy as a result of an audit, will you have the right to contest the auditor's report?

11. *Assignment of the Franchise*

- What are the conditions under which you may assign the franchise to someone else?
- Does the agreement permit you to sell the franchise to someone who meets all the usual qualifications for a franchisee of the company?
- Will the franchisor have the right of first refusal to purchase the franchise if you decide to sell?
- If you should become disabled or die, will your heirs or successors lose all ownership rights to the business?
- If your successors should fail to assign the franchise to someone else within a certain time period, will the franchisor have the right to confiscate the business?
- If the franchisor, for any reason, should confiscate the franchise, what formula will be used to adequately compensate you, your heirs, or successors?
- What are the conditions for operating the franchise as a corporation?

- If the business will be a corporation, does the agreement mandate how much stock you must personally own?
- Will any transfer of stock have to be approved by the franchisor?

12. Renewal

- Will you have the right to renew the franchise agreement when it expires?
- If you do renew the franchise, will you re-execute the same agreement, or will a different agreement be substituted?
- What are the conditions for renewing the agreement?
- Is there a specified period before the expiration date during which you must notify the franchisor of your desire to renew?
- Does the specified period give you enough time to make a decision and comply with the conditions?

13. Termination

- Does the franchisor reserve the right to terminate the agreement unilaterally for any reason?
- Are the stipulated reasons justifiable and appropriate?
- Does your state have laws preventing a franchisor from unilaterally terminating an agreement, no matter what the reason?
- If so, has the franchisor informed you that your state law takes precedence over any provision in the agreement?
- Does the agreement state that your franchise may be terminated in the event of bankruptcy or reorganization due to insolvency?
- Has the franchisor informed you that the Federal Bankruptcy Law prohibits franchisors from terminating an agreement by reason of the franchisee's bankruptcy?
- If the franchisor has the right to terminate the agreement for a default on your part, will you be compensated for your investment?
- If the franchisor should terminate the agreement, will it repurchase any inventory sold to you as part of the franchise arrangement?

14. *Obligations Upon Termination or Expiration*

- What are your obligations upon termination or expiration of the agreement?
- What are your franchisor's obligations?
- If you choose not to renew when the agreement expires, will you have to give up the business?
- Will you have to vacate the premises?
- Will you have to change your business phone number?
- Does the agreement prohibit you from operating a similar business, or one which might be deemed to be in competition, after termination or expiration?
- How long will this covenant not to compete remain in effect?
- Is the time period reasonable, in light of your experience, skills, and ability to maintain a livelihood?

15. *Enforcement and Construction*

- Has an attorney adequately explained the clauses of the agreement relating to severability, substitution, and governing law?
- In the event that a provision of the agreement should be held illegal or unenforceable, will the entire agreement become invalid?
- If a dispute should arise, in which state will it be settled — yours or your franchisor's?

Chapter Thirteen

Dealer's Choice

How to Evaluate a Franchisor

As you probably realize by now, a famous name and a host of locations are no assurance of success in the franchise business. It's true that a franchisor's public exposure and number of outlets add to the benefits of the program, but there are other, often more subtle qualities that may have an even greater influence on your survival.

The Advantages and Risks of Thinking Big

There are trade-offs when you deal with a big franchisor. A large, easily recognized organization is more likely to be well capitalized. Experience shows in a mature franchisor. Many, if not most, of his support staff emerged from the field. Moreover, it's impossible to open five hundred or a thousand outlets and handle their day-to-day headaches without acquiring some very useful know-how.

A major franchise operation has the best public exposure and offers the most potent cooperative benefits to franchisees, particularly advertising reach and purchasing power.

On the opposite side of the coin, a big-time operator is more apt to evolve into a "hot shot" with an inflated self-image and overbearing authority. The best franchisor is the one who guides, not coerces . . . counsels, not commands. There is a natural tendency among franchisors to grow militaristic as their networks swell to nearly unmanageable proportions.

In government, "power corrupts," but in a franchise organization, "power corrodes." Over time, a large franchisor often forgets that his success was borne on the shoulders of numerous franchisees. As a result, he grows more distant from the industry and becomes less and less tuned to the marketplace.

A second risk of selecting a large, rapidly proliferating franchisor is the peril of getting lost in the shuffle. Any company that expands too quickly soon finds itself with more people who have questions than those who have answers. The support staff become diluted with too many priorities. Eventually, the franchisee mortality rate may equal or exceed the recruitment rate.

Consider the case of a famous hairstyling salon that sprang up in 1979 and expanded meteorically to more than 3,000 outlets by the end of 1980. Normally, one would consider such a performance to be a sterling testimonial to entrepreneurial success. Unfortunately, the overextended company declared bankruptcy in 1983 and disappeared from the franchise scene even as the founder's glistening smile adorned the cover of a national business magazine.

The Advantages and Risks of Thinking Small

Simply because a franchisor is small — or just starting to sell franchises — is no reason to discard his offering altogether. However, when there's little history to rely on, your research must be extremely thorough.

It's worth repeating that when people buy franchises, they are looking to replicate the franchisor's own personal success. Nowhere is this quality more pronounced than in the case of the small-time or first-time franchisor. All franchisors started out small, and many insist on staying that way.

An entrepreneur with a successful small business is often goaded into franchising by demand. People walk into the restaurant or store, and ask how they can get into the business themselves. Few, if any, franchisors invest the considerable effort and funds it takes to put together a franchise program without first conducting a painstaking feasibility study. Consequently, although a small franchisor poses somewhat higher risks than a prolific one, the odds are not insurmountable. In fact, a modest organization often provides better one-on-one support.

Experts consider the "ideal" ratio to be one field representative for every twelve franchisees. Beyond that, the level of personal support begins to erode. A small franchisor is often better equipped to handle his franchisee's day-to-day problems. Moreover, he invariably has greater sensitivity toward and rapport with the people in the organization. As a franchisee, you may even have access to the company founder — a benefit essentially unheard of in a large franchise organization.

The main drawbacks to a diminutive franchise chain are less advertising power, which results in higher marketing overhead, and fewer cooperative benefits. You will generally pay higher wholesale prices and invest a greater percentage of your income in advertising. If the franchisor is not well capitalized, you run the risk that the entire program will collapse in an economic downswing or industry slowdown.

Just because a "prototype" business may be successful is no assurance that its success can be replicated elsewhere by others. Often, that success revolves around the genius or skill of its owner, and not on its concept, recognition, or product. Besides that, prototypes don't pay franchise royalties. Deduct from five to fifteen percent from the gross revenues of any business, no matter how successful, and see how much profit it produces (if any). Too many businesses based on concepts that "can't miss" have failed to produce workable franchises. Better to rely on a franchisor with a track record — one who has proved his success can actually be cloned — than one with nothing but a "revolutionary" idea or a "phenomenal" prototype.

The Final Decision

To a franchise marketing director, your decision is just one more sale. But to you, the franchise represents your livelihood and quality of life. Whether or not to franchise — and which franchise to purchase — will be one of the most important decisions you will ever make. Don't make it lightly.

When you evaluate a franchise opportunity, peer behind the glossy color photographs, the meticulously groomed flagship, and the affable smile of the franchisor's representative. Look for signposts from the past telling you about the future.

Just as a franchisor evaluates the qualifications of many franchisees before selecting the right candidate, you should evaluate prospective franchisors according to their "qualifications." Here are some of the important traits to evaluate.

Background Traits

• *Length of time in business*

The longer a franchisor has been in business, the more experience he has to share with you. He knows what works in his line of business. But his "negative" experience is as important as his successes. He knows what *not* to do to be successful: how to avoid the innumerable mistakes, large and small, that characterize a small business when it first starts out.

• *Length of time in franchising*

The longer a franchisor has been involved in franchising, the more capable he is to lead, guide, and motivate the franchise organization. He know what makes franchisees "tick": their ambitions, drives, hopes, and dreams. He knows how to handle problems and stave off crises.

• *Prior litigation or other legal problems*

The fewer lawsuits and legal entanglements a franchisor has had, the more ethical he is likely to be. Favor the franchisor who conscientiously walks the "straight and narrow." Some franchisors have the attitude that a large number of lawsuits is inevitable in the franchise business. But, among other things, legal fees burden the entire franchise organization, eating up funds that might otherwise be spent to the benefit of franchisees.

● *Civil actions/expulsions from securities associations*

A history of civil actions involving fraud or the violation of a franchise law is a red flag for concern. It's true that unscrupulous operators sometimes reform, but unethical business conduct is often part of a lifelong behavior pattern. A slogan heard too often in franchise circles is "anything's legal as long as you get away with it."

Don't take chances. If you have the poor sense to buy a franchise from a convicted felon, or someone who was once expelled from a securities association, you probably deserve whatever consequences befall you.

Industry Know-How

● *Length of time in the industry*

Some franchisors have spent a great deal of time in business, but only a relatively small portion of that time in their current industries. For instance, a franchisor in the electronics industry sold shoes for ten years — twice as long as he has been involved with electronics. Real know-how is derived from real experience.

Give added weight to franchisors who were successful in their own industries *before* they started to franchise.

● *Credentials of the franchise staff*

As you evaluate the backgrounds of the franchisor's staff, compare their credentials to your needs as a franchisee. Are the officers and managers well qualified for their jobs? Is their experience appropriate for the business of the franchise? For example, a franchise sales director might simply be a good sales professional, but the field representative should have abundant experience in the business.

● *Market share or influence*

The greater a franchisor's influence in the marketplace, the greater the cooperative benefits to his franchisees. If a company is dominant in its industry, your franchise may well dominate your local market.

If, for instance, you buy a Hertz car rental franchise, you can be assured the franchisor's market influence will automatically bring you many customers. But if you buy a franchise with little or no share of the national market, you really have no indication of how well the business will do in your area.

● *Advertising reach*

Favor the franchisor that has already conducted national or regional advertising programs that reach customers in your area. When your franchise opens, the public will already know who you are, what you're selling, and why they should patronize your business.

Some franchisors don't conduct advertising campaigns on behalf of their franchisees. If that's the case, you'll end up shouldering the advertising burden yourself. That burden will take a healthy chunk out of your monthly revenues, making it all the more difficult for you to grow.

● *Number of outlets*

Decide whether you'd rather be part of a large franchise chain or a small one. If you're a sharp business person who doesn't need a lot of personal guidance, favor the large organization. Sheer strength in numbers creates powerful cooperative benefits, including national advertising and discount purchasing. If you need or desire personal attention,though, a smaller but established franchisor may be better for you.

● *Net worth*

Give added weight to the franchisor who is well capitalized. In an economic crisis, he is the one who will lead you through the economic waters. As you evaluate the franchisor's net worth, look for the answers to these questions: How much of the asset value of the company represents tangible assets, such as equipment, buildings, and cash on hand?

How much represents intangible assets, such as the value of a trademark or goodwill?

In other words, how much is real, and how much is "fluff"?

● *Past financial stability*

A company that has maintained an even keel through times of economic hardship has extra know-how that may help *you* survive, as well. Give preference to a franchisor whose company has led a life of economic stability, without undergoing numerous re-organizations, mergers, and acquisitions.

● *Cash reserves for handling a crisis*

Study the franchisor's audited financial statement. How much cash does he have on hand? If the amount is not impressive, how many of his assets are convertible — i.e., can be easily liquidated in a crisis?

Give added weight to a franchisor who is prepared to handle cash emergencies if the economy or industry takes an unexpected turn for the worse.

Other Qualifications

● *Quality of training program*

Ask the franchisor for an outline of his training curriculum. Does it touch all the bases? Does it have real substance and value? Think of your initial fee as your tuition to attend the franchise training school, and consider whether the curriculum is worth the price.

● *Franchise operating manual*

Ask to see the operating manual, or, if the franchisor considers it "too secret" to let you browse through, ask to inspect the table of contents. Is the manual comprehensive? Does it provide a complete how-to "bible" for running the business?

• *Level of franchisee satisfaction*

Give preference to franchisors who have the happiest franchisees. Be sure to contact at least three franchisees listed in the franchisor's UFOC. Ask them the questions shown in Chapter Nine of this book under the heading *20. Information Regarding Franchises of the Franchisor.*

• *Management style*

Ultimately, the ideal franchisor is one whose management style and personality blend well with yours. We'll discuss franchisor's management styles in detail in Chapter Fifteen.

The Franchisor Evaluation Worksheet

Once you've considered all these qualifications, you're prepared to evaluate a prospective franchisor's strengths and weaknesses. At this end of this chapter, you'll find a Franchisor Evaluation Worksheet with which to rate each franchisor under your consideration.

This worksheet lists each of the key traits discussed in this chapter. Rate each factor on a scale of 1 to 10 — 1 signifying the lowest rating, 10 the highest. Then multiply your rating by the corresponding weight factor on the right. The result is the "index" for that trait. When you have rated the franchisor on all the traits in the worksheet, add the numbers in the index column. The sum is the franchisor's final "score."

With this evaluation worksheet, there's no set "passing" grade. The worksheet is designed to help you compare the strengths and weaknesses of different franchisors. Before you make a franchise decision, evaluate their scores to find out how each franchisor rates against the others.

Franchisor Evaluation Worksheet

Factor	Weight	Rating	Index

Background

Factor	Weight	Rating	Index
Length of time in business	.10	X _____	= _____
Length of time in franchising	.05	X _____	= _____
Litigation	.05	X _____	= _____
Civil actions	.05	X _____	= _____

Industry Know-How

Length of time in the industry	.05	X _____	= _____
Staff credentials	.05	X _____	= _____
Market share	.05	X _____	= _____
Advertising reach	.05	X _____	= _____
Number of outlets	.05	X _____	= _____

Financial

Net worth	.15	X _____	= _____
Past stability	.05	X _____	= _____
Cash reserves	.05	X _____	= _____

Other

Training program	.06	X _____	= _____
Operations manual	.05	X _____	= _____
Franchisee satisfaction	.06	X _____	= _____
Management style	.08	X _____	= _____

Final Score _____

Section Three

Franchising in Action

"The philosophers must become kings . . . or those who are now called kings must seek wisdom like true and genuine philosophers."

Plato
The Republic

Chapter Fourteen

Capital Ideas

How to Finance a Franchise

Do you want to buy a franchise, but don't have the cash? Fortunately for you, there are a number of ways to finance a franchise investment.

One is the franchisor himself. Almost one out of every five franchisors has a financial assistance program for franchisees. Some of these are willing to finance the entire investment, including real estate, inventory, and working capital. Others will finance only the initial franchise fee.

Where can you find franchisors who finance? One good source is a book called *Franchising for Free*, written by this author and published by John Wiley and Sons. This book provides a detailed, step-by-step guide to creating a franchise financial proposal and a list of more than 250 franchisors who offer financial assistance to potential franchise buyers, organized by category. (You can buy this book at any book store; if you don't find it on the shelves, ask someone to order it.)

Another source is the *Franchise Opportunities Handbook*, published by the Department of Commerce. This book is an exhaustive catalog of U.S. franchisors. To find the ones that offer financial aid, you'll have to pore through every listing. But at least the franchisors are organized by category, so if you're only interested in, say, automotive franchises, you can go right to this section.

You can order a copy by writing to the Department of Commerce, at the following address:

Industry and Trade Administration
Department of Commerce
Washington, DC 20402

Another good source is Info Press, Inc., which publishes *The Franchise Annual*. This catalog lists franchisors as well as franchise consultants. The book sells for $19.95 and can be ordered from:

Info Press, Inc.
Lewiston, NY 14092

Where to Find Financing

The Small Business Administration

Many franchises are started with assistance from the Small Business Administration. To qualify for an SBA-guaranteed loan, you must first be turned down by at least three other sources, usually banks or savings and loans.

The loan is actually extended by a local bank in your trading area, but the SBA guarantees to fulfill your obligations in the event of a default.

The SBA particularly favors franchises because of their high likelihood of success. The best strategy for obtaining an SBA loan is to contact a local loan officer whose bank has experience in SBA-guaranteed financing. Often, independently owned banks have the best SBA departments.

SBIC Investments

Another possible funding source is a licensed Small Business Investment Company (SBIC). This source is an independent venture capital group subsidized by the government to invest in small businesses. An offshoot of this entity is the Minority Enterprise Small Business

Investment Company, or MESBIC, which specializes in loans and grants to minority-owned businesses.

Many SBICs and MESBICs are particularly interested in helping franchise businesses get off the ground.

Venture Capital

If you plan to open several franchises or to sub-franchise, it may be possible to obtain financing from a venture capital group. Each year, venture capitalists invest about $12 billion in more than 50,000 new businesses. Venture capitalists expect a high return on their investments — e.g., two hundred to three hundred percent. Moreover, they want to receive the payout in a short period of time.

When you raise money from a venture capitalist, you must be willing to give up a share of your ownership in the business. The investors will own shares in your company, entitling them to a portion of your profits. Typically, you would also agree to buy back the investors' shares at some point, at a guaranteed price.

For example, let's say you convince a venture capitalist to finance three hotels under a franchise agreement with a world-famous chain. The total investment is $6 million. In return for staking your business, the investment company purchases forty percent of the stock in your corporation. You promise to buy those shares back at the end of four years for the sum of $9 million. As time passes, you distribute profits in the form of dividends,paying out forty percent to your venture partners. Let's say that by the end of the fourth year, you have paid out a total of $9 million in dividends. At that time, you buy back all the stock for another $9 million, as agreed. So, your total payout for the four-year investment amounts to $18 million. The venture group thus realizes a three hundred percent return, and you now own one hundred percent of the business.

The Finance Proposal: A Reminder and Some Helpful Hints

To attract startup money, you'll need a good finance proposal. The financial forecast you created in Chapter Ten provides the core of your plan. But in addition to this realistic snapshot of the business's future performance, create two more plans: a high "optimistic" forecast, and a low "pessimistic" projection.

To create your finance proposal, put the complete forecast together with your resume, personal financial statement, and the franchisor's UFOC. Keep the optimistic and pessimistic plans on hand, in case someone asks to see them; don't include them in your proposal.

If you'd like more information about how to write a successful business plan, the book *Franchising for Free*, mentioned earlier, contains a detailed guide to constructing a successful finance proposal for a franchise business.

The Sources: Choosing the Right One for You

The next step is to locate the right source of funding. Different investment firms tend to specialize in funding certain types of businesses.

To obtain information about licensed Small Business Investment Companies, contact:

> The National Association of SBICs
> 512 Washington Bldg.
> Washington, DC 20005
> (202) 638-3411

This association can supply you with a list of member SBICs in your region. Besides SBA-type investments, many of these firms manage venture capital pools earmarked for small business startups in a diversity of fields.

> To obtain a list of MESBICs nearest you, contact:
> Minority Business Development Agency
> Washington, DC 20230

Venture capital firms actively soliciting new investment targets often advertise in financial newspapers such as *The Wall Street Journal* and *Forbes*. Another good source is a business broker or investment counselor, who may be able to put you in contact with a venture group specifically interested in franchises in your particular industry.

Independent Investors

Besides the big-time venture capital groups, there are also small-time independent investors on the prowl for ripe startup opportunities. Many of these investors are retired or semi-retired executives or military officers. Like the venture capitalist, the independent investor is looking for an attractive payoff and a share of ownership. The two best sources of independent investors are small business brokers and the classified section of your daily metropolitan newspaper. Take your business plan to a business broker (not a real estate or stock broker); he may already know a client looking for just such an opportunity.

Advertising for a partner in the classified section of a newspaper is permissible in most states; however, it's not usually legal to advertise for money. It's absolutely illegal to offer to sell securities — such as stock in your corporation. The best advice is to advertise for a "general manager" with "partnership possibilities."

Selecting a Source: Evaluating the Risks and Rewards

It's best to make telephone contact with a prospective source before sending out your finance proposal. That way, you can quickly determine which ones might be interested, saving yourself the time, money, and aggravation of a wasted mailing.

Using someone else's money always has certain advantages as well as drawbacks. When you evaluate the potential sources for financial assistance, weigh the risks against the benefits before making a final selection. Here are some of the factors to consider.

A Franchisor's Helping Hand

A franchisor who offers financial assistance may make it very easy for you to get into business. If the franchisor believes in your personal credentials, he may be willing to extend more credit than you could get from the bank or some other financial source. Moreover, you might not have to put up any other collateral than the business itself.

Of course, the main reason a franchisor offers financing is to realize additional profits from the interest you will pay on the money you borrow. However, the rates may be more attractive than conventional business loan or mortgage rates.

But when you accept financial assistance from a franchisor, remember that your franchisor will have a lien against your business. In that respect, you are really buying yourself a job, at least until your financial obligation is repaid. Besides royalties, you will have the additional burden of making loan payments to your franchisor. If you default on either, there is always the possibility of the franchisor taking over the business. In contrast, if you finance the business yourself, or through a third party, you will be on firmer ground as a franchisee.

SBA Assistance

The SBA has no other purpose than to help small business owners like yourself get started. When SBA funding is available, you will find the rates extremely reasonable — usually lower than conventional commercial loan rates. Additionally, the SBA may finance more than you could borrow from a bank.

Unfortunately, SBA funding tends to be sporadic. Assistance is not always available, and there are usually lengthy "dry spells" between funding periods. As a result, timing is critical. If your request for assistance does not coincide with a period when funds are available in your area, expect a long wait before your application is considered.

An independent bank or financing company that offers SBA-guaranteed loans is a more reliable source. But you can expect to pay the prevailing interest rate from such sources.

Moreover, the application process can be time-consuming; it might take you from three to six months to receive funding.

SBICs and MESBICs

The main advantage of securing funding from a small business investment company is that, like the SBA, these firms specialize in helping small businesses. Business loans, when they are available, are often offered at lower interest rates than conventional loans.

But, as is the case with SBA funding, SBIC money is not always available. Occasionally, an SBIC will make a direct investment in a small business. The company expects a high return, though, and will normally consider only those franchise investments involving substantialamounts. If you are considering a hotel or a chain of franchises, an

SBIC might be a likely candidate to invest. But if all you have in mind is one outlet in a retail or restaurant chain, you'll perhaps have a hard time interesting an SBIC.

MESBICs are a different story. If you're a minority business owner, you automatically qualify for consideration for a loan, investment, or other assistance from a licensed MESBIC, regardless of the amount you need.

Venture Capitalists

One reason you might want to consider a venture capital group as a source of financing for your franchise is that little or no collateral is required. However, to attract a venture capitalist, you must prepare a plan to open a chain of several franchises. Most of these groups are looking for high returns on their investments and, in most cases, won't be interested in financing a single outlet.

The process of obtaining venture capital is often more stressful than applying for a conventional bank loan. Very likely, you will have to undergo a series of intense interviews and endure a lengthy evaluation period before the group's managers decide.

When you obtain venture capital, you may be staking your entire ownership. If your payout plan doesn't go according to schedule, your investors may have the right to take over the business. Normally, a venture capital group will not want to own more than half of your company; they recognize that the higher your ownership share, the greater your motivation to succeed. But if you fail to make the payout, you may be obligated, under the terms of the investment arrangement, to transfer your fifty percent to the venture group. Remember that your franchisor usually has the right to approve — or disapprove — any assignment of the franchise.

Independent Investors

An independent investor can often provide a fast funding decision. In most cases, you will not have to put up any collateral. But your investor will want an ownership share in the business, probably half.

Remember that any investor in your franchise business must be disclosed to your franchisor, and the investor may be required to meet the same qualifications as any other franchisee.

To help you place all these advantages and drawbacks in perspective, the following list contains questions to ask when you evaluate a source for financing the franchise.

Financing the Franchise: Important Questions

Franchisors

- Does the franchisor you are most interested in offer financial assistance?
- If so, is he willing to finance the entire initial investment?
- Does the amount he is willing to finance include working capital?
- How long will you have to repay the franchisor?
- Is the period within the term of your franchise? Or could you end up having to still make payment seven after the franchise has expired?
- Will there be a large "balloon" payment at the end of the franchise term? If so, will you be able to handle it?
- Will you have to put up any other collateral besides the business itself?
- If you default on your loan payments, will you be in violation of your franchise agreement as well?
- Can the business handle the monthly payments and still make a decent profit?

Small Business Administration

- Is direct SBA assistance available in your locality at this time?
- If not, are any local banks offering SBA-guaranteed business loans?
- Has your application already been turned down by at least three conventional lending institutions?
- Are the interest rates favorable, compared to conventional commercial loan rates?

- How long will it take to process your loan application? Will you receive the funds before the deadline stipulated in your franchise agreement for opening the outlet?

SBICs

- Is funding from an SBIC available in your area at this time?
- Does the SBIC lend money or invest in firms in your line of business?
- Does the SBIC lend or invest in franchises?
- Is the amount you need sufficient to interest the investment company?
- How does the interest rate compare to a conventional loan rate?
- How long will it take the SBIC to make a decision?
- Will you receive the funds before the deadline stipulated in your franchise agreement?

MESBICs

- Are you a member of any officially recognized minority?
- Is there a MESBIC in your area?
- If so, are funds currently available for minority-owned enterprises?
- Have you answered all the questions under "SBIC" above?

Venture Capitalists

- Is the amount you need sufficient to interest a venture capital group?
- Are you willing to give up part of your ownership in the business for a period of time?
- How much will you have to pay out to the investors? Can the business handle it?
- How long will it take the venture capital group to make a decision? Will you receive the funds before the deadline stipulated in your franchise agreement?

Chapter Fifteen

The King and You

The Chemistry of Franchising

A franchise is more than a ready-made business format, a system of success secrets, and a continuous financial relationship. When you franchise, you are franchising more than a business: you're franchising your future and, possibly, that of your family and heirs. From a franchisor, you expect guidance, assistance, and troubleshooting from a qualified representative. But in addition to know-how, you wish to derive esteem, independence, and personal satisfaction. And, let's face it, you also want to have fun.

Remember that a franchise requires more than a financial commitment: its formula involves intellectual and emotional commitments, too. If you are evaluating a franchise offering, you should seek that exquisite chemistry in which all these complex relationships are subtly balanced.

The Franchisor's Profile

Just exactly who are these people who want to sell us their franchises and lead us trustingly into the jungle of entrepreneurship?

Before you entrust your business and family to one of these interesting, but often eccentric, pathfinders, you would be well advised to know the nature of the beast.

The typical franchisor is, first of all, an over-achiever. Often, his success is circumstantial. While certain of his traits and ambitions separate him from the crowd, many franchisors indisputably become successful in spite of themselves.

As a business strategy, franchising is so powerful that it may propel a franchisor well beyond his initial notions of success. Few of today's franchise millionaires ever imagined they would reach such heights. Often, they were propelled beyond not only their wildest dreams but also their maximum level of competency. Small wonder that a franchisor's minor personality quirks become grossly exaggerated, or that he tends to become convinced of his own infallibility.

It would be very unfair to lump all franchisors into a single stereotype. But most, either consciously or not, fall into one of three basic types, which we'll call the Hot Shot, the Philosopher-King, and Our Father Who Art in Headquarters.

The Hot Shot

Franchisors invariably excel at selling. Their individual sales styles and philosophies are extensions of their personalities. Some are low-key and educational, others loud and persuasive. The franchise Hot Shot is energetic, enthusiastic, and highly sales oriented. To him, the world is simply a subset of some all-encompassing entity called Sales. He is the keeper of time-worn cliches, the most likely to conclude a meeting with the platitude, "You only have to remember three things to be successful: sell, sell, sell!"

Hot Shot's hallmark is promotion. His franchise company devotes an enormous share of its operating budget to advertising, public relations, and marketing. The recruitment program is typified by slick presentations, lavish audio-visuals, and emotion-charged gatherings. Hot Shot feels more at home in a crowded auditorium than sitting behind a desk in an office cubicle. The organization is apt to be relatively informal, with a loose "think-tank" approach to decision making.

In person, Hot Shot is bubbly, talkative, and fast moving. He gestures broadly, speaks rapidly, and has something to say on every topic. He has obvious difficulty sitting still or standing in one place more than a few seconds at a time.

Hot Shot is prone to using everyday analogies to explain things. He is especially keen on food analogies. For instance, he might compare a franchise to a loaf of bread, a budget to a pizza. You'll also hear him express his ideas as automobiles or airplanes or a bucket of water.

He is always on the move and goes to great lengths to make you aware of his harried schedule. The reason he is so busy is that he insists on handling every minute detail of his operation himself. He doesn't delegate very well; while he trusts his own judgment, he has less faith in that of his subordinates.

By reason of his exaggerated success, every franchisor tends to believe in his own infallibility. Like getting vaccinated, one should experience just enough failure to become immune to its devastating effects. A franchisor who has tasted little from the cup of failure operates in a bubble of self-perceived invulnerability.

Who, you might wonder, would buy a franchise from a motor-mouthed, self-indulgent Hot Shot? The answer is obvious: another fast-talking, energetic sales professional. Personality quirks aside, Hot Shot is above all a successful franchisor, and his aggressive, sales-oriented business style contributed largely to that success.

A Hot Shot promoter is not the franchisor for every franchisee; but if he is surrounded by competent technicians, Hot Shot just might be the right "topping on the pizza" for the seriously sales-minded franchisee.

The Philosopher-King

Like the successful Hot Shot, a Philosopher-King franchisor has grown to believe in his infallibility. Each step he has taken, every decision he has made, has always been right on the money. As a result, he has become blinded to the fact that his success is rooted in the combined efforts of loyal and talented subordinates. He sees only himself standing on the tip of an ever-expanding pyramid and assumes that his unique superiority catapulted him there. Whereas success was side-lined near Hot Shot's mouth, it proceeded directly to Philosopher-King's head.

Philosopher-King alternates between low-key reserve and high-energy confrontation. He is a ceaseless problem solver and the most likely of all franchisors to be a chronic workaholic. His franchise organization is highly structured and neatly defined, probably modeled after some favorite corporate giant.

Unlike Hot Shot, he gladly, even adamantly, delegates responsibility. He knows, of course, that he can do everyone's job better than they can, but he also realizes the perils of spreading himself too thin. Consequently, he imposes his authority by issuing mandates, policies, and philosophical edicts.

His organization has a written "company goal," not to mention a "service objective" and "management philosophy." Though his subordinates make their own decisions, they must constantly apply Philosopher-King's policies and sayings to every situation.

Viewing himself as an innovator, he is not above experimenting with ideas or campaigns. He fills his private time by reading management textbooks and business articles. His office has a bulletin board where he pins up clippings from magazines like the *Harvard Business Review* or excerpts from books like *Future Shock* or *Theory Z.*

Philosopher-King has a "power" vocabulary, often tinged with technological or scientific allusions. He doesn't phone colleagues, he "networks" with them. He issues periodic bulletins containing his reflections on the company or the customer or the meaning of life.

He leads by instruction, not inspiration or example, and envisions himself as a kind of untouchable guru around whom franchisees gather and thirst for knowledge. Because he believes in his infallibility, he is a ruthless authoritarian.

Still, like Hot Shot, Philosopher-King is exactly the right franchisor for many franchisees. He is the "thinking man's" franchisor, the mentor of entrepreneurs. His know-how is carefully and meticulously documented and, because it enhances his self-image, he gladly divulges his secrets to his loyal followers.

Don't overlook the fact that his confidence, inquisitiveness, and above-average intelligence were critical ingredients in his success. Undoubtedly, some of it rubs off on his franchisees.

Our Father Who Art In Headquarters

The comforting poise of the franchise father figure seems almost out of place when contrasted with the energetic earthiness of a Hot Shot and the confident pithiness of a Philosopher-King. Our Father

Who Art in Headquarters is a veritable fountain of stability, grace, and wisdom.

Father is low key. He smiles a lot, often in lieu of commenting or replying. It's a quiet, knowing kind of smile, almost condescending. Above all, he caters to the franchisee's desire for an experienced, understanding authority. He is an object of respect, as reinforced by his graying temples and balding pate. Father speaks simply and forthrightly, using few words but exuding common sense.

He delegates authority better than any of his counterparts. He knows his limitations as well as his strengths. He is the most likely to be a risen-from-the-ranks franchisor, a former blue-collar laborer or kitchen helper. He does not have an extensive educational background, but makes up for it with an ample supply of wisdom pearls.

Father is uncommonly polite; he practices being likeable in front of a mirror when no one is watching. He glows with warmth and trustworthiness, the kind of executive who puts his arm around your shoulder or clasps your hand with both of his in a handshake. Pictures of his family — not just one or two, but dozens — adorn his desk, possibly even the walls. He has a fondness for nostalgia and decorates his office with antiques rather than paintings.

The father figure is sometimes motherly: the wise and kindly founder who baked the first cookie or blended the first spaghetti sauce, or plucked the first chicken. Regardless of gender, Our Father Who Art in Headquarters is the franchisor who understands the franchisee's longing for security and direction.

Apart from the Crowd

In spite of their quirks, most franchisors share some important qualities. We all know somebody who's loud and energetic, or self-centered and philosophical, or warm and fatherly. But not many of these folks are the heads of multimillion-dollar business empires.

Franchisors are ambitious, confident, and tireless. They are also risk takers. Originally, each one set out on his own with little more than a fervent desire and a lucid vision of the future. Some had more financial backing than others, but all of them threw the dice at some crucial turning point in their careers. A franchisor is something very close to a complete entrepreneur. Unlike his franchisees, he has a varied repertoire of the skills and know-how it takes to start a business and make it successful. America's franchisors are among the original two in ten independent business owners who actually survive.

When you acquire a franchise, you are presumably acquiring your franchisor's blueprint for success. All other factors being equal, the ideal franchisor is the one whose management style and personality match your needs. A successful franchisor is one who carefully and equitably balances the varied and intricate relationships that underlie the franchise contract, the one who recognizes that his franchisee's success is ultimately his own.

Chapter Sixteen

Franchising and Your
Tax Status

Mark H. was impressed by the financial projections of the Ultimate Earnings Franchise Corporation. When he checked the figures for himself he verified that by meeting all the sales goals, his business could easily clear $75,000 per year. He foresaw re-investing some of those profits in bigger inventories which in turn would increase his future profits.

By the time corporate taxes were deducted from the company's profits and his personal income taxes were paid, Mark was shocked to discover that his actual take-home pay turned out to be about half that amount. With a few intelligent tax strategies, he could have increased the after-tax profits of the business by almost twenty percent.

The idea of tax planning is not to cheat the government out of its fair share of your company's income, but rather to maximize your ability to thrive in a competitive capitalistic economy. As your business grows, the government benefits from increased tax revenues and a healthier economic atmosphere.

When the President signed the 1986 Tax Reform Act into law, the nation's tax laws — and tax liabilities — instantly and dramatically changed. For individuals, the law meant real reform in how their tax liability is computed. But for businesses in general, and franchises in particular, the law represented a tax revision more than a tax reform.

One of the most significant effects was to decrease the corporate tax rate, making it somewhat more desirable to operate the franchise as a corporation. Franchise agreements were affected by changes in the handling of trademark licenses and acquisitions. In addition, the 1986 law changed how equipment purchases and construction costs are handled. In this chapter, we'll explore these changes and their implications for the tax liability of your franchise business.

Personal vs. Corporate Income

The 1986 Tax Reform Act decreased tax rates for both individuals and corporations. As a result, the law affects a basic filing status decision — whether to conduct the franchise business as a sole proprietorship, partnership, or corporation.

When a business is operated as a sole proprietorship or partnership, the business income is considered the personal income of the owner or partners. In other words, the profits of the business are reported as ordinary income and taxed at the rate for individuals. Prior to 1987, there were as many as fifteen different tax brackets for individuals, depending not only on income but on marital and filing status as well. As of 1988, only two individual tax rates applied: 15% of the first $29,750 of taxable income, and 28% of the taxable income above that amount. However, there is an additional 5% surcharge for especially high personal income levels. For instance, a single person must pay both the 28% income tax plus a 5% surcharge for income between $43,150 and $89,560. Another surcharge applies to taxable income above $89,560. For couples, the surcharge pertains to incomes falling between $71,900 and $149,250.

Besides the tax rate, the amount of taxable income paid by individuals will also decline; the standard deduction taken by individuals who do not itemize deductions will increase. For a single head of household, the standard deduction will have ascended to $4,400 by 1988, and for couples, $5,000.

When a business is operated as a corporation, its income is taxed twice. First, corporate income tax is levied on the corporation itself. Second, after-tax profits distributed to shareholders are taxed as personal income.

The 1986 tax law created five official corporate tax rates:

- Amounts under $50,000   15% ($7500 at the
                                                   $50,000 level)

- Amounts from $50,000-75,000 $7500 plus 25% of the
                                                   amount over $50,000
                                                   ($13,750 at the $75,000
                                                   level)

- Amounts from $75,000-100,000 $13,750 plus 34% of the
                                                     amount over $75,000
                                                     ($22,250 at the $100,000
                                                     level)

- Amounts from $100,000-335,000 $22,250 plus 34% of the
                                                       amount over $100,000,
                                                       plus a surcharge of 5% or
                                                       $11,750 on that amount,
                                                       whichever is less
                                                       ($91,650 at the $335,000
                                                       level)

- Amounts over $335,000 $91,650 plus 34% of the
                                                   amount over $335,000

Both individuals and corporations must pay an alternative minimum tax, or AMT, instead of their normal income tax, if the AMT turns out to be higher. How do you know which to pay? To figure the AMT, first multiply your taxable income times twenty percent. Then subtract a flat exemption of $40,000. (The exemption is less if your taxable income is $150,000 or more). Add to this figure the amount of corporate tax preference items, such as depreciation, installment sales, capital gains (corporations only), and contributions to charity involving appreciable property. The result is your AMT. If this figure is higher than the income tax you would otherwise have to pay, you must pay the amount of the AMT instead.

Of course, there are other considerations besides taxation which affect your decision to operate the business as a proprietorship, partnership, or corporation. The owner of a proprietorship, or partners in a partnership, are generally responsible for the liabilities of the business. The company's debts are literally the owner's personal debts. In contrast, a corporation is a separate entity. The shareholders may not be liable for the corporation's debts.

Trademarks and Trade Names

Prior to 1986, the tax law allowed businesses to amortize costs related to trademark registrations over a period of five years. For example, you could deduct the expenses of having an advertising agency design a logo, registering the logo with the federal government, or suing someone for infringement.

The 1986 Tax Reform Act did away with this deduction. As a result, you may not deduct an amount for obtaining a trade name license with the purchase of a franchise.

If you signed your franchise agreement prior to March 1, 1986, you can continue to amortize any expenses relating to trademarks and trade names, if you spent five percent of the total amount (or one million dollars, whichever is less) prior to that date.

In other words, most franchisees who signed agreements before then may still be able to amortize any future costs they incur in connection with a registered trademark.

Equipment Purchases

As of 1986, the tax law did away with one of the most important business incentives of the former tax code, the investment credit. Previously, businesses could claim a deduction for investing in property, such as equipment and machinery placed into service during the tax year. Now, to claim a deduction, you must depreciate the cost of equipment purchases.

Depreciation is computed over a "recovery period" which determines the amount of each year's deduction. For example, if a business buys a piece of equipment with a recovery period of seven years, it may claim a deduction for depreciation for seven years. The amount depreciated each year is determined from a schedule.

The recovery period for equipment such as motor vehicles, computer hardware, or copy machines is five years. A seven-year recovery period is specified for items like furnishings and fixtures.

An alternative to depreciation is "expensing out." The law permits small businesses to deduct the entire cost of new equipment purchased during the tax year, up to a maximum of $10,000. But, if you elect to expense out an equipment purchase, you may not also claim a deduction for depreciation.

When you purchase a franchise and develop a new outlet, it may be advantageous to depreciate rather than expense out the cost of business equipment, including vehicles. Here's why: A typical franchise business will not turn a profit until at least its second year of operation. Except in rare circumstances, it is unlikely that a new outlet will earn a profit in its first year. In other words, its taxable income will be zero; hence, a large number of deductions will be unnecessary. By expensing out, you realize a deduction that would be irrelevant.

If you elect to expense-out the purchase of equipment, furnishings, and fixtures, you will not be able to depreciate these items in later years when you may need a deduction to reduce the company's taxable income.

Note that an equipment purchase may be expensed out only in the year in which it was acquired. However, depreciated equipment results in a deduction every year until the recovery period has been fulfilled.

Inventory is not subject to depreciation or expensing. The cost of inventory purchases, including non-inventory items you intend to sell to others, *must* be capitalized by the business.

Real Estate

Today's tax law makes real estate investing somewhat less desirable than it was in the past, particularly for a franchise outlet. Before 1986, real estate could usually be depreciated on an accelerated basis, resulting in a proportionately larger deduction in the initial years following the acquisition.

Business property must now be depreciated over 31.5 years, without accelerated recovery. That means an amount equal to about 3.15% of the real estate purchase price may be deducted every year. The real impact of the new depreciation rules will be to suppress real estate values, making a property purchase less attractive as part of a franchise investment.

Tax Treatment Evaluation Chart

Below is a Tax Treatment Evaluation Chart to help you devise a tax strategy for your franchise business. This chart lists typical items in an initial franchise investment and shows how they may be treated under the current tax law.

Tax Treatment Evaluation Chart

Item	Treatment
Initial Franchise Fee	List as an asset on the books of the business. Normally, no deduction may be claimed.
Lease	Amortize over the length of the lease.
Real estate purchase	Depreciate over 31.5 years, regardless of the terms of the purchase.
Fixtures and improvements	Depreciate over 7 years (or expense out in the tax year of purchase).
Motor vehicles	Depreciate over 5 years.
Computer hardware/ office equipment	Depreciate over 5 years.
Opening inventory	List as an asset on the books of the business. Normally, no deduction may be claimed.

Appendix A

Where to Find Franchise Opportunities

Where to Find Franchise Opportunities

Business Journals

Wall Street Journal
22 Cortland St.
New York, NY 10007

Forbes
60 Fifth Ave.
New York, NY 10011

Barron's
22 Cortland St.
New York, NY 10007

Info Franchise Newsletter
736 Center St.
Lewiston, NY 14092

Franchise Directories

Franchise Opportunities Handbook
U.S. Government Printing Office
Washington, DC 20402

The Franchise Annual
Info Press
736 Center St.
Lewiston, NY 14092

Franchise Yearbook
2311 Pontius Ave.
Los Angeles, CA 90064

Franchising for Free
John Wiley & Sons
Business/Law/General Books Division
605 Third Ave.
New York, NY 10158

Magazines

Venture
35 W. 45th St.
New York, NY 10036

Entrepreneur
2311 Pontius Ave.
Los Angeles, CA 90064

Franchise Expositions

Q.M. Marketing
1515 West Chester Pike, Ste. B-2
West Chester, PA 19382

Appendix B

Sample Franchise Agreement

Franchise Agreement

1. Grant of Franchise

A. Widget World Franchise Corporation (the "Franchisor") hereby grants to Franchisee a license to use the trade name "Widget World" and the trade marks associated therewith, and a franchise to operate a Widget World outlet (the "Outlet") in the geographical market identified in an exhibit to this agreement.

B. Franchisee shall use the trade name and marks in the sale of widgets and widget-related goods, and franchisee's place of business shall be known only as "Widget World."

C. The name of any corporation operating this franchise may include the words "Widget World" or any other trade mark owned or licensed by franchisor, but only with the written consent of franchisor.

2. Exclusive Territory

Franchisor shall not, while this agreement is in force, conduct a similar operation, or grant a similar franchise to any other franchisee, within the territory defined in Exhibit ___.

3. Term

This agreement shall continue for a period of ten (10) years from the date hereof, and shall be automatically renewed for an additional ten-year term, unless at least six (6) months before the expiration of this agreement, franchisee gives to franchisor notice in writing of termination at the end of the term.

4. Development and Opening

Within ninety (90) days following the execution of this agreement, franchisee shall do or cause the following to be done:

A. Secure all financing required to develop the outlet;

B. Complete all arrangements for a site for the outlet. Franchisor shall have the right and option to approve the selected site prior to the development and opening of the outlet;

C. Execute a lease for the premises in which the outlet shall be operated, and deliver to the franchisor a true and correct copy;

D. Obtain all licenses and permits required to conduct the business;

E. Obtain all improvements, fixtures, supplies, and inventory.

5. Payments

A. Franchise Fee

Franchisee shall make payment to franchisor of _____ Dollars ($_____) upon the execution of this agreement, receipt of which is hereby acknowledged. In return for this payment, franchisee shall receive the right to do business as a licensed Widget World franchisee under the terms of this agreement, and to receive the services and assistance hereinafter set forth. The initial fee shall be fully earned by franchisor and is nonrefundable.

B. Continuing Royalty

Franchisee shall, on the tenth (10th) day of each month, pay to franchisor the sum equal to   percent (%) of the net sales of franchisee for the preceding month. As used in this agreement, the term "net sales" shall include all sales made by franchisee pursuant to this agreement, but shall not include any sums collected and paid out for any sales or excise tax imposed by any duly constituted government authority.

C. Advertising Fee

Franchisee shall pay to franchisor as an advertising fee the sum equal to   percent (%) of franchisee's monthly gross sales. The sum shall be paid on or before the tenth (10th) day of each month and shall be based on the net sales of the month preceding the date of payment. The amount of franchisee's net sales shall be determined in the same manner as that specified in subsection B of this section, above.

D. Interest Penalties

If franchisee fails to remit the payments required under subsections A through C of this section, above, all amounts which franchisee owes to franchisor shall bear interest after due date at the highest applicable legal rate.

6. Advertising

A. Franchisee agrees to use all advertising designs, materials, media, and methods of preparation prescribed by or which conform to franchisor's standards and specifications.

B. Franchisee shall refrain from using any advertising designs, materials, media, and methods of preparation which do not meet with franchisor's standards and specifications.

C. Franchisor shall make available to franchisee any assistance that may be required, based on the experience and judgment of franchisor, in the design, preparation, and placement of advertising and promotional materials for use in local advertising.

D. Franchisor shall administer the Franchisee Cooperative Advertising Fund, and direct the development of all advertising and promotional programs. The content of the advertising, as well as the media in which the advertising is to be placed and the defined advertising area, shall be at the discretion of the franchisor.

7. Trade Marks

A. Franchisor shall make available to franchisee franchisor's trade names and marks. For the purpose of this agreement, "the marks" shall be defined as all symbols, logos, trade marks, and trade names owned and/or under application by franchisor.

B. Franchisee agrees that its rights to use the marks are derived solely from this agreement, and franchisee shall not derive any right, title, or interest in the marks, other than a license to use them in connection with the franchise outlet while this agreement is in force.

C. Franchisee shall use the name and service marks only in such manner as prescribed by franchisor and in no other way.

D. Franchisee shall immediately notify franchisor of any apparent infringement of the use of the marks.

E. If it becomes advisable at any time in franchisor's sole discretion to discontinue or modify the use of any mark, franchisee agrees to comply within a reasonable time after notice thereof by franchisor.

8. Products, Supplies, and Equipment

Franchisee understands and acknowledges that every detail of the franchise system is important to franchisor, to franchisee, and to other franchisees to develop and maintain high and uniform standards of quality, cleanliness, appearance, services, products, and techniques, and to protect and enhance the reputation and goodwill of the franchise system. Franchisee accordingly agrees:

(1) To use all materials, supplies, goods, uniforms, fixtures, furnishings, signs, equipment, methods of exterior and interior design and construction, and methods of production and preparation prescribed by or which conform to franchisor's standards and specifications.

(2) To refrain from using or selling any products, materials, supplies, goods, uniforms, fixtures, furnishings, signs, equipment, and

211

methods of production which do not meet with franchisor's standards and specifications.

(3) To offer for sale any such products as shall be expressly approved for sale in writing by franchisor, and to offer for sale all products that have been designated as approved by franchisor.

(4) To maintain at all times a sufficient supply of approved products.

(5) To purchase all products, supplies, equipment, and materials required for conduct of the franchise operation from suppliers who demonstrate, to the reasonable satisfaction of franchisor, the ability to meet all of franchisor's standards and specifications for such items; who possess adequate capacity and facilities to supply franchisee's needs in the quantities, at the times, and with the reliability requisite to an efficient operation; and who have been approved, in writing, by franchisor. Franchisee may submit to franchisor a written request for approval of a supplier not previously approved by franchisor.

9. Standards and Procedures

A. Management Standards

Franchisee agrees to comply with franchisor's standards with respect to product preparation, merchandising, employee recruitment, training, equipment, and facility maintenance.

B. Personnel Standards

Franchisee shall hire only efficient, competent, sober, and courteous employees for the conduct of the business, and shall pay their wages, commissions, and other compensation with no liability therefor on the part of the franchisor. Franchisee shall require all employees to comply with franchisor's standards for grooming and appearance.

C. Best Efforts

Franchisee agrees to devote his/her best efforts to the operation of the outlet and to the supervision of its employees. Franchisee agrees that it will not engage in any other business activity which may conflict with the obligations of this agreement or impair the operation of the outlet.

D. Insurance

Franchisee shall, at his expense, procure and maintain in full force and effect during the entire term of this agreement, comprehensive public, fire damage, product and motor vehicle liability insurance in the amount of _____ Dollars ($_____) for each person and _____ Dollars ($_____) for each occurrence for bodily and personal injury, death and property damage. Fire damage insurance shall be sufficient to cover repair or replacement of all equipment, inventory, tools, and supplies normally required to operate the outlet, as specified in franchisor's operating manual. Franchisor shall be named as an additional insured under all such insurance policies, as its interests may appear, and contain a waiver by the carrier of all subrogation rights against franchisor. Maintenance of insurance under this paragraph shall not relieve franchisee of liability under the default provisions set forth in this agreement.

10. Training and Assistance

A. Franchisor agrees to make personal training facilities available to franchisee, to furnish an operating manual, to make promotional and other recommendations, and to furnish franchisee, at franchisee's place of business, a trained supervisor for not less than three (3) days during the initial six-day period of franchisee's operation.

B. Franchisee shall, at franchisee's expense, attend franchisor's training program at a place to be designated by franchisor prior to the opening of the outlet. During the term of this agreement, franchisee may send one other designee through the same program, at franchisee's expense. Franchisee agrees to pay any travel and living expenses which may be incurred by franchisee and/or his other designee in connection with the training program.

213

C. Franchisor shall loan to franchisee for the term of this agreement an operating manual containing the standards, specifications, procedures, and techniques of the franchise system, and may, at its sole discretion, revise, from time to time, the contents of the manuals, incorporating new standards, specifications, procedures, and techniques.

D. Franchisor agrees to furnish franchisee with the following:

(1) guidelines and approval for the location of a suitable site for the outlet. By providing such guidelines and approval, franchisor in no way promises, warrants or otherwise represents that the site location is the optimal location for the outlet;

(2) assistance in negotiating a lease for the outlet, when appropriate;

(3) assistance in planning the layout of the outlet;

(4) assistance in the conduct of a Grand Opening promotion for the outlet.

11. Business Conduct

A. All representations made by franchisee to others shall be completely factual. Franchisee agrees to abide by all laws, regulations, and codes.

B. Franchisee agrees to protect, defend, and indemnify franchisor and to hold franchisor harmless from and against any and all costs, expenses, including attorneys' fees, court costs, losses, liabilities, damages, claims and demands of every kind or nature, arising in any way out of the occupation, use or operation of any fixtures, equipment, goods, merchandise, or products used or sold at the outlet.

C. Franchisee will not divulge any business information, whether written or oral, received from franchisor or from any meetings of other of franchisor's franchisees, until such time as disclosure to the public may be required by the nature of the information. Such information may include, but is not limited to, promotional material or plans, expansion plans, new products, marketing information, costs or other financial data.

12. Reports and Inspections

A. Franchisee agrees to furnish to franchisor, within thirty (30) days after the end of franchisee's fiscal year, a full and complete statement in writing of income and expense for the outlet during the preceding year. The statement shall be prepared in accordance with accepted accounting standards and practices by an independent accountant or auditor and certified by the accountant or auditor to be correct.

B. Franchisee agrees to open his books and records to the inspection of franchisor, provided, however, that franchisee shall have been given reasonable advance notice. Franchisee agrees to cooperate fully with representatives of the franchisor making any such inspection. In the event an understatement of net revenues for the period of any audit is determined by any such audit, franchisee shall reimburse franchisor for the cost of such audit or inspection.

13. Relationship of the Parties

A. Franchisee shall be an independent contractor, and nothing in this agreement shall be construed so as to create or imply a fiduciary relationship between the parties, nor to make either party a general or specific agent, legal representative, subsidiary, joint venturer, or servant of the other.

B. Franchisee is in no way authorized to make a contract, agreement, warranty or representation on behalf of franchisor or to create any obligation, express or implied, on behalf of franchisor.

C. Franchisee shall be responsible for his/her own taxes, including without limitation any taxes levied upon the outlet.

215

14. Assignment of Franchise

Franchisee's rights in the franchise may be assigned only as follows:

A. Upon franchisee's death, the rights of franchisee in the franchise may pass to franchisee's next of kin or other beneficiaries, provided that such next of kin or other beneficiaries agree in written form satisfactory to franchisor to assume all of franchisee's obligations under this agreement.

B. Franchisee may sell his interests in the franchise to another party, provided that the following conditions are met:

(1) the assignee is of good moral character, meets franchisor's normal qualifications for franchisees of franchisor, will comply with franchisor's training requirements, and enters into any and all direct agreements with franchisor that franchisor is then requiring of newly franchised persons;

(2) all monetary obligations of franchisee hereunder are fully paid, and franchisee executes a general release of all claims against franchisor, its officers and directors;

(3) The assignee pays franchisor for its legal, training, and other expenses in connection with the assignment;

(4) franchisee has first offered to sell his franchise to franchisor upon the same terms as the purchaser has offered franchisee in writing, and franchisor has refused the offer or failed to accept it for a period of thirty (30) days;

(5) franchisee shall reaffirm a covenant not to compete in favor of franchisor.

C. Franchisee may assign and transfer his rights hereunder to a corporation without, however, being relieved of any personal liability, provided that the following conditions are met:

(1) the corporation is newly formed and shall conduct no other business but the franchise business, which shall continue to be managed by franchisee;

216

(2) franchisee owns the controlling stock interest in the corporation and is the principal executive officer thereof;

(3) the articles of incorporation, by-laws and other organizational documents of the corporation shall recite that the issuance and assignment of any interest therein is restricted by the terms of this agreement, and all issued and outstanding stock certificates of such corporation shall bear a legend reflecting or referring to the restrictions of this agreement;

(4) all stockholders of the corporation guarantee, in written form satisfactory to franchisor, to be bound jointly and severally by all provisions of this franchise agreement;

(5) franchisee shall not use any mark in a public offering of his securities, except to reflect his franchise relationship with franchisor.

15. Termination

If franchisee defaults under the terms of this agreement and such default shall not be cured within thirty (30) days after receipt of written notice to cure from franchisor, then, in addition to all other remedies at law or in equity, franchisor may immediately terminate this agreement. Termination under such conditions shall become effective immediately upon the date of receipt by franchisee of a written notice of termination. Franchisee shall be considered to be in default under this agreement if:

(1) franchisee fails to open the business within the time specified in Section 4 of this agreement, above;

(2) franchisee abandons the franchise;

(3) franchisee attempts to assign this agreement without prior written approval of franchisor;

(4) franchisee misuses or makes an unauthorized use of the mark in a manner which materially impairs the goodwill of franchisor;

217

(5) franchisee has made a material misrepresentation to franchisor before or after being granted the franchise;

(6) franchisee discloses or reproduces any portion of the franchisor's operating manual to any unauthorized party;

(7) franchisee fails to abide by his covenant not to compete as provided in this agreement;

(8) franchisee fails to comply substantially with any of the requirements imposed upon franchisee by this agreement.

16. Rights and Obligations of the Parties Upon Termination or Expiration

A. On termination or expiration of this agreement, franchisee shall do or cause to be done the following:

(1) promptly pay all amounts owed to franchisor which are then unpaid;

(2) immediately cease to use any and all marks and names, and any other trade secrets, confidential information, operating manuals, slogans, signs, symbols, or devices forming part of the franchise system or otherwise used in connection with conduct of the franchise outlet;

(3) immediately return to franchisor all advertising materials, operating manuals, plans, specifications, and other materials prepared by franchisor and relative to the franchise system.

B. Covenant Not to Compete

Franchisee, its officers, directors, and shareholders agree during the term of this agreement, or upon expiration or termination, or non-renewal for any reason, they shall not have any interest as an owner, partner, director, officer, employee, manager, consultant, shareholder, representative, agent, or in any other capacity for any reason for a period of two (2) years after the occurrence of said event(s) in any business or activity involving the retail sale of widgets or proposing to engage in the sale of widgets.

Franchisee acknowledges that this covenant is reasonable and necessary and agrees that its failure to adhere strictly to the restrictions of this paragraph will cause substantial and irreparable damage to franchisor. Franchisee hereby acknowledges, therefore, that any violation of the terms and conditions of this covenant shall give rise to an entitlement to injunctive relief.

17. Enforcement and Construction

A. Severability

The paragraphs of this agreement are severable, and in the event any paragraph or portion of the agreement is declared illegal or unenforceable, the remainder of the agreement shall be effective and binding on the parties.

B. Notice

Whenever, under the terms of this agreement, notice is required, the same shall be deemed delivered if delivered by hand to whom intended, or to any adult person employed by franchisee at franchisee's place of business, or upon deposit in any U.S. depository for mail delivery, addressed to franchisee or franchisor at their respective principal business addresses.

C. Specific Performance

Nothing contained herein shall bar the franchisor's or franchisee's right to obtain specific performance of the provisions of this agreement and injunctive relief against threatened conduct that will cause it loss or damages, under customary equity rules, including applicable rules for obtaining restraining orders and preliminary injunctions.

D. Governing Law

This agreement is entered into and shall be construed in accordance with the laws of the state of _____, as of the date of execution of this agreement.

219

E. Successors

This agreement shall inure to the benefit of and be binding upon the executors, administrators, heirs, assigns and successors in interest of the parties.

Appendix C

Sample Uniform Franchise Offering Circular

INFORMATION FOR PROSPECTIVE FRANCHISEE — REQUIRED BY FEDERAL TRADE COMMISSION

To protect you, we've required your franchisor to give you this information.

We haven't checked it, and don't know if it's correct.

It should help you make up your mind. Study it carefully. While it includes some information about your contract, don't rely on it alone to understand your contract. Read all of your contract carefully.

Buying a franchise is a complicated investment. Take your time to decide. If possible, show your contract and this information to an advisor, like a lawyer or an accountant.

If you find anything you think may be wrong or anything important that's been left out, you should let us know about it. It may be against the law.

There may also be laws on franchising in your state. Ask your state agencies about them.

FEDERAL TRADE COMMISSION
Washington, D.C.

1.
The Franchisor and Any Predecessor

The Franchisor

Widget World Franchise Corporation is a California corporation incorporated on July 1, 1981. Its affiliate, Widget World, Inc., was first organized in March, 1972 as a sole proprietorship under the name California Widgets, and was incorporated on November 1, 1976. Widget World, Inc. today does business under its own name and under the name California Widgets. The franchisor maintains its principal business offices at 2001 Odyssey Street, San Francisco, California 94010.

Franchisor's Business

Widget World Franchise Corporation is a franchising company which grants franchises and trains, advises, and assists franchisees in the establishment and operation of retail outlets known as Widget World Stores. Franchisor's primary activities are education, market planning, advertising, consulting, and coordination of product distribution for its franchisees.

The franchise business is a retail business engaged in the merchandising and sale of widgets and related products and services, utilizing the franchisor's systems, procedures, and trade marks. The primary customers for the outlet are individuals purchasing widgets for recreational use and education, and business customers purchasing widgets for planning, reference, and decorative uses.

The franchisee will have to compete with independent widget dealers and company-owned outlets operated by major widget manufacturers.

Prior Business Experience of the Franchisor and Predecessors

John J. Johnson, president of Widget World Franchise Corporation and its affiliate, has operated a retail widget store similar to the business to be operated by the franchisee since March, 1972.

Neither the franchisor, its affiliate nor principals have offered any other franchises in any line of business. Widget World Franchise Corporation has been offering franchises since February, 1983.

2.
Prior Business Experience of Persons Affiliated With Franchisor: Franchise Brokers

John J. Johnson President Widget World Franchise Corporation	From March, 1972 until the present, Mr. Johnson has operated a retail business, as sole proprietor of California Widgets from 1974 until November, 1976, and as president of Widget World, Inc. from November 1976

until the present. He has been president of Widget World Franchise Corporation since its formation in July, 1981.

William W. Wilhelm
Vice President
Widget World
Franchise Corporation

From 1975 until May, 1981, Mr. Wilhelm was president and general manager of GadgetCo in Sacramento, California. He joined Widget World, Inc. in May, 1981 as general manager. He has been vice president of Widget World Franchise Corporation since its formation in July, 1981.

Alice A. Allison
Vice President
Widget World
Franchise Corporation

From June, 1979 until January, 1981, Ms. Allison was the marketing director for Great American Gizmos. She joined Widget World in January, 1981 as vice president of marketing. She has been vice president of Widget World Franchise Corporation since its formation in July, 1981.

Edward E. Edwards
Secretary-Treasurer
Widget World
Franchise Corporation

From May, 1978 until the present, Mr. Edwards has been a public accountant. He has been secretary-treasurer of Widget World Franchise Corporation since its formation in July, 1981.

Martin M. Martin
Franchise Director
Widget World
Franchise Corporation

From April, 1977 until October, 1984, Mr. Martin was Franchise Marketing Director for Specialty Retailers Franchises, Inc. He joined Widget World Franchise Corporation as Franchise Director in October, 1984.

There are no franchise brokers affiliated with franchisor.

3.
Litigation

Neither the franchisor nor any other person identified in Item 2 above has any administrative or material civil action (or a significant number of civil actions irrespective of materiality) pending against them alleging a violation of any franchise law, fraud, embezzlement, fraudulent conversion, restraint of trade, unfair or deceptive business practices, misappropriation of property, or comparable allegations, other than a pending proceeding involving the arrest of such a person.

Neither the franchisor nor any person identified in Item 2 above has during the 10-year period immediately preceding the date of this offering circular been convicted of a felony or pleaded *nolo contendere* to any felony charge or been held liable in any other civil action or other legal proceeding where such felony, civil action, complaint or other legal proceeding involved violation of any franchise law, fraud, embezzlement, fraudulent conversion, restraint of trade, unfair or deceptive practices, misappropriation of property or comparable allegations.

Neither the franchisor nor any person identified in Item 2 above is subject to any currently effective injunctive or restrictive order or decree relating to the franchise or under any federal, state, or Canadian franchise, securities, antitrust, trade regulation or trade practice law as a result of a concluded or pending action or proceeding brought by a public agency; nor is subject to any currently effective order of any national securities association or national securities exchange (as defined in the Securities and Exchange Act of 1934) suspending or expelling such persons from membership in such association or exchange.

4.
Bankruptcy

During the 15-year period immediately preceding the date of the offering circular neither the franchisor nor any predecessor, current officer or general partner of the franchisor has been adjudged bankrupt or reorganized due to insolvency or been a principal officer of a company or a general partner of a partnership within one year of the time that such company or partnership was adjudged bankrupt or reorganized due to insolvency or is otherwise subject to any such pending bankruptcy or reorganization proceeding.

5.
Franchisee's Initial Franchise Fee or Other Payment

The full franchise fee is payable to franchisor upon execution of the franchise agreement. The franchise fee is placed with the other general funds of the franchisor and is non- refundable unless franchisee shall fail to successfully complete the training program required by the franchisor. In that event, the franchisor will refund 50% of the franchise fee, the balance to be retained by the franchisor to cover accounting, legal and training costs.

The initial franchise fee is $

6.
Other Fees

A royalty fee of % of net revenues is payable monthly by the franchisee. This amount is calculated on the basis of actual cash receipts paid by customers less sales, excise or other taxes collected, and is payable to franchisor by the 10th of each month. Franchisor offers a training program in or in another location which may be centrally situated among a number of franchisees scheduled to attend the training session, if deemed advisable in the discretion of the franchisor. While there is no additional charge for the training, franchisee is required to pay the expense of transportation to and from the training program and all food and lodging expenses while attending. Costs for room and board, depending on the specific location of the training session, might be $75 per day per person.

7.
Franchisee's Initial Investment

The initial investment may vary according to franchisee's choice of site, method of business organization, inventory levels and improvements. Following is a summary of estimated initial investment requirements for a low and high investment:

Estimated Initial Investment

Item	How Paid	Low	High	When Due	Paid To
Initial Fee	Lump sum	$17,500	17,500	Signing of Agreement	Franchisor
Supplies	As ordered	2,500	3,200	As ordered	Supplier(s)
Equipment	As ordered	5,500	6,500	As ordered	Vendor(s)
Lease Deposits	As agreed	5,000	7,500	As agreed	Lessor
Fixtures	As ordered	13,300	17,900	As ordered	Vendor(s)
Utilities	As agreed	1,000	1,500	As agreed	Supplier(s)
Leasehold Improvements	As agreed	3,300	6,200	As agreed	Vendor(s)
Initial Inventory	As ordered	45,000	60,000	As ordered	Supplier(s)
Working Capital (1)	As incurred	30,000	45,000	As incurred	Various
Totals		$123,100	165,300		

(1) Working capital includes grand-opening advertising and start-up promotional expenses.

Franchisor does not offer either direct or indirect financing to franchisee for any item. Franchisee must obtain his own financing, if needed, and should be aware that the availability and terms of financing will depend on factors such as the availability of financing in general, the credit-worthiness of the franchisee, other security the franchisee may have, policies of lending institutions concerning the type of business to be operated by the franchisee, and so forth.

There are no other direct or indirect payments in conjunction with the purchase of the franchise.

8.
Obligations of Franchisee to Purchase or Lease from Designated Suppliers

Franchisee is not obligated to purchase or lease any products or services or classes of products or services from any designated source. At franchisee's option, franchisee may purchase selected inventory items from franchisor, or from franchisor's list of suppliers, but is under no obligation to purchase any item from either the franchisor or any recommended supplier.

9.
Obligations of Franchisee to Purchase or Lease in Accordance with Specifications or from Approved Suppliers

Franchisee is required to purchase all of the fixtures and initial inventory specified in franchisor's operating manual, in conformance with franchisor's specifications relating to quality, design or other similar standards.

Franchisee is required to purchase or cause to be purchased certain advertising literature for use in promotion of the franchise outlet. These items may be purchased in printed form from franchisor at a price equal to franchisor's actual printing cost plus 10%. If franchisee elects to have these materials printed by another source, the printed materials must be of equal quality to those offered by franchisor and must contain only the art, photographs and wording approved by franchisor.

Franchisee is obligated by the Franchise Agreement to purchase business liability, comprehensive and fire/damage insurance in the amount of $1,000,000 combined single limit and $3,000,000 per occurrence for business liability, and fire/damage coverage sufficient to repair or replace all equipment, tools, inventory and supplies essential to the operation of the franchise business. Neither the franchisor nor its affiliate will or may derive profits from the required purchase of equipment or supplies except for equipment or supplies made available by franchisor.

10.
Financing Arrangements

Neither the franchisor nor its affiliate offer financing directly or indirectly, or arrange or guarantee financing for franchisees. There are no payments received by franchisor or its affiliate from any person, lending institution or other source for its placement of financing with such person, lending institution or other source.

There is no past or present practice of the franchisor to sell, assign or discount to a third party any note, contract or other obligation of the franchisee in whole or in part.

11.
Obligations of the Franchisor; Other Supervision, Assistance or Services

Upon execution of the franchise agreement and prior to the opening of the franchise business, it is the obligation of the franchisor to:

1. designate an exclusive territory;

2. provide a training program at a time designated by franchisor prior to the opening of the business;

3. provide a list of specifications, standards, and suppliers for inventory, equipment and supplies;

4. provide guidance in methods, procedures, techniques and operations in the form of an operating manual and other printed materials, and

5. provide camera-ready artwork for printed materials to be used by franchisee in the conduct of the franchise business.

There is no other supervision, assistance or service to be provided by the franchisor prior to the opening of the franchise business pursuant to the franchise agreement or otherwise.

Upon commencement of the business, franchisor is obligated to:

1. protect the exclusive territory by assuring that no other franchises or company-owned outlets are granted or established therein;

2. modify the operating manual as required to improve or update the systems and procedures;

3. provide ongoing assistance and guidance by personal visits to the franchise outlet by authorized personnel of the franchisor;

4. administer a cooperative advertising fund to conduct advertising and promotions in selected media as deemed appropriate, and

5. provide on-site assistance in opening and operating the outlet for at least ten business days at the time of the grand opening.

There is no other supervision, assistance or service to be provided by the franchisor during the operation of the franchise business pursuant to the franchise agreement or otherwise.

Franchisor does not select the location of the franchisee's business, but must approve the location prior to the franchisee's commencement of the business. Franchisor, at no charge, provides guidelines for site selection. Pursuant to the franchise agreement, franchisee is obligated to complete all of the required tasks necessary to commence the franchise business within 90 days after execution of the agreement.

A training program is provided by franchisor at its principal offices, or at another location to be designated by franchisor. The training program consists of map industry training, product knowledge, selling techniques, marketing strategies, competitive overview, customer knowledge, advertising techniques, business management, expansion strategies, promotional methods, inventory planning, and merchandising techniques and methods. The training program must be successfully completed prior to the opening of the franchise business. While there is no charge for the training, franchisee may be required to pay for all transportation and lodging expenses incurred by attending the training. No additional training programs are available as of the date of this offering circular. Franchisee may repeat the program if he desires to do so.

12.
Exclusive Area or Territory

Franchisor grants to franchisee during the term of the franchise an exclusive area (franchised territory). Neither the franchisor nor its parent or affiliates will establish other franchises or company-owned outlets using the franchisor's trade marks or by leasing similar products or services under a different trade mark or name, in the designated territory.

A designated territory is exclusive to the franchisee for the length of the franchise and is not altered by achievement of a certain sales volume, market penetration or other contingency. Other than the territory granted by the agreement, franchisee may obtain any other territory only by executing a separate franchise agreement. A franchisee's sub-franchising rights within the exclusive territory granted by the agreement would be subject to the following conditions:

1. franchisee meets all applicable standards and complies fully with all applicable state and federal laws, rules and regulations relating to the offer and sale of franchises and to sub-franchising;

2. franchisee will pay to franchisor the then-standard initial franchise fee for each sub-franchise sold by franchisee;

3. franchisee will pay to franchisor the then-standard royalty fee for the aggregate earnings of all sub- franchises sold by franchisee in the exclusive area;

4. all sub-franchisees of the franchisee will meet all applicable qualifications and standards for franchisees of the franchisor, and execute the franchisor's standard franchise agreement, and

5. all sub-franchisees of the franchisee must complete the franchisor's training program for franchisees prior to commencement of the sub-franchise business.

13.
Trade Marks, Service Marks, Trade Names, Logotypes and Commercial Symbols

Widget World Franchise Corporation has applied for a trade mark registration on the Principal Register of the U.S. Patent and Trademark Office for the following:

14.
Patents and Copyrights

Franchisor owns no special patents that pertain to the offering.

Franchisor and its principals possess proprietary know-how in the form of trade secrets, operating methods, specifications, technique, information and systems in the operation of retail map stores and in the merchandising of products and services. The know-how is disclosed in part in the copyrighted operating manual which franchisee receives solely for the purpose of developing the franchise and for the term of the agreement.

15.
Obligation of the Franchisee to Participate in the Actual Operation of the Franchise Business

Franchisee is not obligated to participate fulltime in the operation of the franchise business. However, if franchisee opts not to participate fulltime, a qualified manager must be in the employ of the franchise business and must have completed the franchisor's training program. Travel, room and board, and salary of the manager would be at the expense of franchisee.

16.
Restrictions on Goods and Services Offered by Franchisee

Pursuant to the franchise agreement, the franchisee may not offer any classes of products or services not approved by franchisor. Franchisor does not stipulate the specific brands, makes or suppliers of goods and services.

Franchisee may not own an interest in, perform any business activity on behalf of, or be in the employ of another retail map business. Franchisee is not limited in the customers to whom he may solicit the sale of goods and services.

17.
Renewal, Termination, Repurchase, Modification and Assignment of the Franchise Agreement and Related Information

The term of the franchise agreement is ten years and is not affected by any agreement other than the franchise agreement.

Upon expiration of the initial term, if the franchisee is in compliance with all the provisions of the agreement, franchisee shall have the option to renew for an additional term by notifying the franchisor of its intention to renew six months prior to the expiration of the franchise and by executing a new franchise agreement and supportive agreements as are then customarily used by the franchisor. No fee is charged for renewal of the franchise.

If, upon expiration, the franchisee is in default of the agreement or fails to renew the franchise agreement within thirty (30) days following the expiration, the franchise will be deemed terminated.

The franchisee may terminate the franchise if franchisor does not fulfill its obligations under the agreement. Franchisee may terminate by exercising its option to sell the franchise to a fully disclosed and approved purchaser.

Franchisor may terminate the franchise if franchisee fails to open the business within 90 days following the signing of the agreement, if

233

franchisee fails to pass or complete the training program, or if franchisee is in default of the agreement and fails to cure such default within thirty (30) days of notice. Further, the franchisor may terminate the franchise if franchisee abandons the franchise, becomes insolvent or bankrupt (to the extent permitted by the Federal Bankruptcy Law), is convicted of or pleads no contest to a felony or crime involving moral turpitude, or makes an unauthorized assignment of the franchise, discloses any trade secrets of the franchisor,or has an interest in or engages in a business activity competitive with the franchise, except to the extent permitted by the California Franchise Relations Act, if franchisee is located in California.

The California Franchise Relations Act (Business and Professional Code Sections 20000 to 20043, effective January 1, 1981) provides additional rights to California franchisees concerning termination and non-renewal. No franchise may be terminated except for good cause, and franchisee must be given a notice of default and a reasonable opportunity to cure defaults (except that for certain defaults specified in the statute, no notice or cure is required by law). The statute also requires that notice of any intention by a franchisor or sub-franchisor not to renew a franchise agreement be given at least 180 days prior to the expiration of a franchise agreement. In the event that any of the provisions of the franchise agreement conflict with this statute, the offending provisions will be considered invalid.

Upon termination or expiration, franchisee is obligated to pay franchisor within 15 days any amounts that are due and unpaid for products or services, cease to identify himself as a franchisee, return all advertising materials, forms, stationery or other printed matter bearing franchisor's trade marks, cancel all fictitious name permits, business licenses or other permits relating to the franchise, notify the telephone company and other listing agencies of the termination, honor the non-compete covenant — which may or may not be enforceable in California — and return all manuals and written communications to the franchisor. Franchisee would thereafter have no interest in or rights to the franchise business.

If franchisee notifies franchisor that it desires to sell any interest in the franchise, franchisor has the right at its sole discretion to repurchase the franchise. Further, should the franchisee obtain a bona fide written offer from a responsible and fully disclosed purchaser, franchisor would have the right at its discretion to purchase the interest for the same price and on the same terms and conditions as contained in the offer. Franchisor shall have 30 days from the receipt of notification of intent to sell to exercise its right of first refusal to repurchase the franchise.

With prior approval of franchisor, franchisee may assign its assets and liabilities to a newly formed corporation that conducts no other business than the franchise and in which franchisee owns and controls not less than 60% of the equity and voting power, and for which franchisee personally guarantees all performance, obligations and debts created by the franchise agreement.

Except as set forth in the above paragraph, none of the ownership of the franchisee may be voluntarily, involuntarily, directly or indirectly assigned, sold, subdivided, sub-franchised or otherwise transferred by franchisee without prior written approval of franchisor. In the event of an approved assignment, other than to a corporation controlled by franchisee, assignee must pay to franchisor a transfer and retaining fee equal to 50% of the initial franchise fee. The approved assignee must pass the training program and execute the then-current franchise agreement.

The agreement may not be modified or amended except by mutual consent and execution of a written instrument. Franchisor is not restricted from transferring the franchise agreement or from designating any subsidiary, affiliate or agent to perform any and all acts franchisor is obligated to perform. Franchisor has the right to modify the operating procedures and specifications of the franchise, but has no right to modify the terms of the agreement subsequent to its signing. Upon death or disability of the franchisee or the principal owner, the executor, administrator or other personal representative must assign the franchise to a fully disclosed and approved person who meets the standard qualifications for franchisees of the franchisor. If such assignment is not made within 90 days after the death or disability, the failure to transfer the interest in the franchise would constitute a breach. Notwithstanding the above, at any time subsequent to the death or disability of the franchisee or principal owner, franchisor may obtain an interim manager to run the business until such assignment is made.

Franchisee agrees by signing the franchise agreement that it will not engage in any business or activity competitive with the franchise for a period of one year from the date of termination or expiration of the franchise. However, such a covenant may or may not be enforceable in the State of California, under the laws of California.

235

18.
Arrangements with Public Figures

Franchisor does not give or promise any compensation or other benefit to any public figure arising in whole or in part from the use of any public figure in the name or symbol of the franchise or the endorsement or recommendation of the franchise by any public figure in advertisements.

No arrangements have been made by franchisor under which the franchisee may use a public figure. Franchisee is wholly unrestricted in its use of public figures in its advertisements and promotions, with the exception that, pursuant to the franchise agreement, printed materials, including endorsements, must be approved in advance by franchisor.

19.
Actual, Average, Projected or Forecasted Franchise Sales, Profits or Earnings

Since these are the first franchises offered, the franchisor presents no statements, oral or written, or other indications of actual, average, projected or forecasted sales, profits or earnings.

20.
Information Regarding Franchises of the Franchisor

Four franchises have been sold and are operational as of the effective date of this offering circular:

Thomas Thompson
Widget World by the Bay
520 Bay Ave.
San Francisco, CA 94010
(415) 555-0000

Carla Carlson
Napa Widget World
18512 Hwy. 19
Napa, CA 93313
(707) 555-2222

Lars Larsen	David Davidson
Southland Widget World	Midland Widget World
910 Straightline Blvd.	2221 Plainview Dr.
Los Angeles, CA 90010	Sacramento, CA 91119
(213) 555-6616	(916) 555-8828

No franchises have been cancelled, terminated, refused renewal, or re-acquired by repurchase or otherwise by franchisor.

Franchisor estimates that it will grant franchises as follows during the one-year period following the date of this offering circular:

State	Number of outlets
California	5
Florida	2
Illinois	2
Kansas	1
New York	3
Texas	3
Washington	1

21.
Franchisor's Financial Statements

Attached are the most recent audited financial statements of the franchisor.

22.
Agreements

Attached is a copy of the franchisor's franchise agreement and all related contracts and agreements.

Appendix D
Suggested Reading

_____, *Are You Ready for Franchising?*, Small Business Administration, Washington, D.C., 1974.

_____, *Franchise Annual, The*, Info Press, New York, 1986.

_____, *Franchising in the Economy, 1985-86*, U.S. Dept. of Commerce, Washington, D.C., 1986.

_____, *Franchise Opportunities Handbook*, U.S. Dept. of Commerce, Washington, D.C., 1986.

Foster, Dennis L., *Franchising for Free*, John Wiley & Sons, New York, 1987.

_____, Foster, Dennis L., "Franchising: A Successful Growth Strategy in the Modern Economy," *Executive*, 1982.

_____, Foster, Dennis L., "Franchising: Strategies for the Third Wave," *Computer Dealer*, 1983.

_____, Foster, Dennis L., "Franchising in the Computer Industry," *Computer Dealer*, 1981.

_____, Foster, Dennis L., "Price Fixing," *Computer Dealer*, 1980.

Glickman, Gladys, *Franchising*, Matthew Bender, New York, 1976.

Henworth, Banks and Ginalski, William, *How to Franchise Your Business*, The Franchise Group, Inc., Phoenix, 1981.

Modica, Alfred, *Franchising: Get Your Own Business and be Your Own Boss for under $5000*, Quick Fox, New York, 1981.

Rudnick, Lewis, *Franchising and the Law*, American Franchise Association, Washington, D.C., 1979.

Seltz, David, *How to Get Started in Your Own Franchise Business*, Farnsworth Publishing, New York, 1967.

Vaughn, Charles, *Franchising*, D. C. Heath, Lexington, Mass., 1974.

Index

C

D

E

245

R

S

V

W